Suddenly Single

WIDOW'S EDITION

Navigating Grief While Colliding With Purpose

Jan Mitchell

© Copyright 2022

IBG Publications, Inc.

Jan Mitchell

IBG PUBLICATIONS
Putting the POWER in your pen!

Published by I.B.G. Publications, LLC, a Power to Wealth Company

Web Address: WWW.IBGPublications.Com

admin@IBGPublications.Com / 904-419-9810

Copyright, 2022 by Jan Mitchell

IBG Publications, Inc., Jacksonville, FL

ISBN: 978-1-956266-40-5

Mitchell, Jan
SUDDENLY Single: Widow's Edition-Navigating Grief While Colliding With Purpose.

All rights reserved. This book or its parts may not be reproduced in any form, stored in a retrieval system, or transmitted in any form, by any means-electronic, mechanical, photocopy, recording or otherwise, without prior written permission of the publisher or author, except as provided by the United States of America Copyright law.

Printed in the United States of America.

SUDDENLY *Single* WIDOW'S EDITION

Dedication

I dedicate this book to all widows and widowers. Losing your spouse is one of the greatest challenges you will or have ever faced in life. It's not easy moving forward after such a great loss.

I know. I've been there.

However, I want to encourage you that there is still LIFE, JOY, PEACE, LOVE & HAPPINESS after this. You will survive. You will have peace and comfort again. Keep reading and be inspired.

I dedicate this book to my family who walked through this journey of Steve's death with me: Nathaniel Stansberry and Christeen Morris-Stansberry (my parents). To my three beautiful, strong, worthy, and intelligent daughters: Ava, Zian & Korii; my siblings: Teddy/Sophie (my sis-in-love), Chrissy, Juli, and Nathan.

Thank you for every phone call or text to check on me, the food, blankets, and many acts of love you showered on me, Steve, and the girls throughout the entire journey and beyond.

To my daughters, you are strong and resilient. I love you.

To my church family, Freewill Outreach Ministries-Indianapolis, Pastor Hail & Lady Geri Louis, Ms. Mary Harris, Shauna Dixon and to all the saints and friends who showed up: thank you for being there and keeping me grounded while I was going through one of the roughest seasons of my life. Your visits to the hospital and encouraging calls as well as making sure that I stayed focused was a godsend. I love you and will never forget your kindnesses.

I dedicate this book to the late, Elder Stephen Lee Mitchell (Steve). You were a good husband and you taught me how to love. Thank you for the love that you embraced me and my girls with, making us all a family.

We appreciate and miss your love, boisterous laughter, and presence. You will forever be ingrained in our hearts.

Last, but always first, I dedicate this book to God. You are the One who gave me the strength and resilience that I needed for this journey. Thank you for gracing me with Your love, strength, and joy throughout this process. I cannot do anything without Your Spirit guiding me every day.

Thank you for blessing me to experience the beauty of marriage. Thank you for bringing Steve into me and the girls' lives and allowing us to experience what real love was through him. We're forever indebted to You.

HEAL AND LIVE!

Jan Mitchell

SUDDENLY *Single* **WIDOW'S EDITION**

TABLE OF CONTENTS

DEDICATION.. 3
WELCOME... 9

CHAPTER I: The Beginning........................... 13
CHAPTER II : Grief Is Not Linear Nor Is
        It A Life Sentence 35
CHAPTER III: Money & Other Matters........ 57
CHAPTER IV: Surviving The Firsts............... 65
CHAPTER V: Drama & Forgiveness.............. 75
CHAPTER VI: Widow's Fire.......................... 91
CHAPTER VII: Another Chance At A Happy
        Ending...................................... 109
CHAPTER VIII: Rediscovering You In A New
        Season: Healed, Whole & Moving
        Forward.................................... 123

POEM: Self-Worth Awakening....................... 155
REFERENCES... 157

Jan Mitchell

About the Author.. 161

Contact The Author.. 163

SUDDENLY *Single* WIDOW'S EDITION

Welcome

Jan Mitchell

Welcome!

I know that hardly sounds like a "pleasant" greeting when you think of the surrounding circumstances that brought you to pick up this book.

I get it.

It was hard for me to write, as I knew that I would have to revisit places that, to be honest, I'd rather forget. But not my beloved spouse, Steve, of course; He will always hold a space in my heart and memories.

"SUDDENLY Single: Widow's Edition," was meant to be an anthology, a collection of various stories sharing multiple perspectives of the widow/er's life, not just *my* story.

As this is a sensitive subject, I decided to pen this first book alone because my aspiration in writing this book is to infuse HOPE and encouragement to other widows and widowers, young, old, and in-between.

In addition, I wrote this book to encourage those who felt unworthy of marriage the first time and concluded that this was their only chance at love. It doesn't matter if you had one year of marriage before your spouse passed or were blessed with fifty. We now find ourselves "SUDDENLY Single," and we need to know how to navigate this painful, and sometimes

SUDDENLY *Single* WIDOW'S EDITION

confusing journey. A part of my healing journey was writing this book.

Do you feel encouraged to share your story? If so, I hope **YOU** will join me in SHARING your account in "SUDDENLY Single: Widow's Edition, Vol. II."

If interested, contact me via my personal email address at: jan.mitchell35@yahoo.com.

Much love,

Jan Mitchell

P.S. Please stay connected as I launch my non-profit organization, *She Moves Forward, Inc.,* in the spring of 2023.

This organization will provide a safe space for widows to find hope and equip them with the tools & resources they need to move forward holistically.

Jan Mitchell

CHAPTER I:

The Beginning

How in the HELL did I end up back here? A single, *youngish* mother, with not only one, but now three daughters and one granddaughter.

I was reliving my earlier years. Yet, in a different sense. No, perhaps, in the same sense, but with a more mature perspective. Let me rewind ten years.

"You're going to be married and it's going to happen this year."

The year happened to be 2011. I was sitting in the middle of a Chinese buffet with two ladies: my mentor, a powerful and prophetic woman of God and the church mother.

When I heard these words, my mouth fell open. I had subtly listened to the Holy Spirit whisper the exact words just a few months earlier. Many years ago, I thought I had "heard God" state that someone else would be my spouse. Well, I discovered that I was wrong. Due to this, I was afraid to share with the current ladies that this confirmed what I had recently heard. I wanted to avoid being wrong again. However, this time was different from the last time. Last time, there was no confirmation that what I desired was God's desire for me.

I couldn't believe what I was hearing. I had given up on marriage and trusting God for this particular area of my life. I had concluded that I would remain a single Mom with my two daughters for the rest of my life. After all, I concluded that if God could help me stay "pure" and stay "busy" in ministry and all my other responsibilities, I'd be just fine. In my mind, I didn't "*need*" marriage. Or at least, that's the lie I told myself to appease the fact that I did not feel *worthy* of marriage.

It was easier to accept that lie than acknowledge the painful places in my life where I had not yet surrendered to the Father's healing grace. I felt I had made too many mistakes to "qualify" to be a wife. Yes, even after giving my life to Christ.

Often, I vacillated between "religion" and "relationship" to drive my walk with Christ. I had experimental knowledge of God's goodness towards me. However, when it came to my love life I didn't think He cared.

Paul explains in **Galatians 5:6**, *"For in Christ Jesus neither circumcision nor uncircumcision has any value. The only thing that counts is faith expressing itself through love."* (NIV)

What you believe about God will determine how you relate to Him.

I had prayed earlier at the start of 2011 and advised God, "I don't see marriage happening for me, so, if

Jan Mitchell

You can just help me to stay abstinent, we'll be doing just fine."

As a young believer, I often battled with I living a completely abstinent life, even as a believer. I had many days of success and several days of failure.

On the nights that I was successful, it was because I had spent that night crying out to God, asking Him to keep me and not allow me to give in to the strong urge that I would often have, especially on the days before my menstrual cycle. On those days, it felt as if my libido would leap over walls and run through troops.

Literally.

Or I would pray to God, asking Him to allow me to fall asleep quickly so I could "sleep away" the pressure. He would graciously answer me each time. I'd wake up the following day refreshed and guilt-free. It may sound *silly* to some, but it worked for me! Yet, as I began to grow in self-awareness, I learned to manage these temptations...most days.

I also tried to be careful of guarding myself against external factors that would arouse sexual desire. I realized that as a single person seeking to rebuild and maintain sexual integrity, I had to put healthy boundaries in place.

SUDDENLY *Single* WIDOW'S EDITION

I mention "I had to" because often, we find ourselves doing things to meet others' expectations versus honoring God and ourselves. Growing up in the church, we were made to believe that maintaining sexual purity was a goal that would be "rewarded" with a husband. Marriage was looked at as a "prize" for abstaining from sex. Virginity and purity are highly regarded; however, due to not having "balanced" teaching on sexual integrity, many fell short of this standard. Others who consistently "passed the test" often became self-righteous against those who didn't.

I am not perfect nor proclaim to have passed **every** test. So, even though I had "fallen" a few times and asked God for forgiveness, I still carried a shame that made me feel *unworthy* to "qualify" as a wife. I was holding several leadership positions in the church and still struggled with self-acceptance, forgiveness, and self-love.

I was not yet renewed in my mind about who I was in Christ's eyes and how much He loved me. I was "moving forward" in ministry, but deep inside, I did not feel good about myself because of past sins. The "fruit" of toxic purity culture teaching abstinence is for something other than honoring God and self = shame & self-loathing.

Now, many years later, I was receiving the confirmation of what I had heard earlier: *I was going to become a wife*! I knew nothing about being a wife as I had not previously been married to my girls' father. I had my first children in my early and mid-20s. They are both nine years apart (The age difference was not planned). Ironically, Steve and I were also nine years apart in age.

He was older.

* * *

Sitting at the table, trying to gather my thoughts, I could hardly contain my excitement. I erupted with many questions:

"Did God say who it is?"

"Oh my God, are you serious?!

"How do you prepare to be a wife?!"

*"Did He say **who** it is?!"*

We all laughed joyfully. The announcement ruined the rest of my appetite as I was too excited to finish eating.

This was it.

The moment that I had prayed for.

The last time I thought that a particular guy was going to be my husband, I found out that I was wrong and ended up with a broken heart.

SUDDENLY *Single* WIDOW'S EDITION

This guy and I had developed a friendship expanding over three years. We traveled together, went out in group settings together, did ministry together. Most importantly, he loved *God*. He had rich, chocolate skin with deep-set dimples.

Lord, have mercy!

But he wasn't "the one."

During our friendship, I had developed a crush on him. But because of fear of rejection, I kept silent.

Real love dispels fear.

I kept silent because I wanted to maintain a friendship with him and be as close to him as I could. I didn't want to risk *pressuring* him at the risk of *losing* him. I accepted that any time in his presence was "good enough" for me.

But it came at the expense of losing me.

And it wasn't his fault because we always have a choice. I did not have to settle for breadcrumbs & scraps when I was the King's daughter. But, I had yet to receive and believe who I was.

Maintaining silent about my true feelings and not seeking wise counsel landed me with a bruised heart.

I was so convinced that he was going to be the one that I rejected other prospects, even without the promise of this man's heart. Thankfully, there was never any physical intimacy between us.

So, when I overheard from a mutual friend and relative that he wasn't interested in me because he didn't want a "ready-made" family, it crushed me.

He had known all along how I felt about him. He wasn't "into me" but lacked the courage to tell me. I could have accepted him being straightforward with me versus being brushed off with a religious cliché. Before this knowledge, there were times I would attempt to tell him how I felt, but he would always brush it off by saying, "Well, let's see what God says." This response kept me waiting to see what God would say to him about us.

I needed to seek clarity for myself.

Well, waiting to "see what God would say" didn't produce anything. I heard this man's thoughts about our relationship through this family member.

Leaving the restaurant, I could hardly contain myself. I let out shrieks of joy as I drove home. While I was excited, I didn't have any close friends with whom to share the news. I had developed a friendship with a new guy at our church named Steve, who had recently divorced and was also the Pastor's nephew, but I wasn't going to tell him.

SUDDENLY *Single* WIDOW'S EDITION

So, I shared with my work team and general manager that I would be getting married. When they heard the news, I was met with many congratulations followed by, "What's his name?", and "We didn't know that you were dating anyone, Jan."

I answered, "I'm not dating anyone at this time. So, I don't know *his name*, but I'm getting married this year!" We all laughed.

I knew they thought I was crazy at that moment, but I didn't care. I was exercising my faith. I had no idea who my husband would be, yet I took God at His word and began preparing myself.

My excitement and confidence eventually trickled over to my manager and colleagues. One particularly rough night at work, my manager called me to his office. As he began encouraging me about the evening's events, he reminded me, "Don't be too upset about it, Jan, and keep your head up. Do you know why? Because you're getting married this year!"

I pointed at "Jim" and said with a big grin, "You're right!" We both laughed.

* * *

While I anticipated the fulfillment of God's promise to me, I began to study the Bible on what a godly wife looks like and how she behaves. I would often hear my Pastor preach over the pulpit, "If you want to be a wife, you've got to start carrying yourself like a wife."

Well, what did that mean? What did that look like? I'd never been a wife before. One obvious meaning was that being a wife meant being devoted and single in heart to one man. It meant presenting myself in a way so that not just any and every man had access to me, whether physically, emotionally, or spiritually. A faithful and godly wife is trustworthy. That trust is built by her actions and developing good character prior to marriage; her outward beauty is not enough. How could I add value to this man's life and mine? What value would I bring to the table?

Every man should not have access to you when you're preparing to be a wife.

"Her husband has full confidence in her and lacks nothing of value. She brings him good, not harm, all the days of her life." **(Proverbs 31:11-12**, NIV)

Becoming a wife doesn't just happen when you say, "I do." Having wifely qualities is cultivated long before the proposal.

She's a woman who has prepared herself emotionally, physically, spiritually, financially, and psychologically. She's content with who she is before she becomes a

SUDDENLY *Single* WIDOW'S EDITION

wife. She understands that before genuinely loving another, she must be able to love herself first.

I had to learn how to love and honor myself before I became a wife. I began to understand that a man couldn't and didn't complete me, but rather that I was already "whole" in Christ. My identity and everything that made me had been established from birth when God created me. Marriage and my husband would be an added blessing and "benefit" to my life, not the overall meaning of life.

* * *

During a particular season of abandonment from Christ, I had entertained a relationship with a married man. I spiraled down a dangerous path of perversion, which landed me into many addictions. This affair started shortly after my heart broke over the relationship I thought would be with my longtime friend.

It began with a compliment on a day I was hurting the most. "Thomas" called me as he had noticed that my countenance had fallen when I came to church. He knew something had transpired between the friend and me.

As I began to pour out my story, which was a trap from Hell, "Thomas" felt the "need" to encourage me. While he was encouraging me, I could hear Holy

Spirit whispering, "It's nice that he's encouraging you; however, he AND HIS WIFE need to be on this phone encouraging you."

I didn't realize it at the time, but I was full of spiritual pride & I was self-righteous. I felt that since I had a few years of abstinence under my belt and had conquered a few of my struggles, I was "above this".

In my arrogance, I advised Holy Spirit that I wasn't even attracted to the man AT ALL and could handle it. Well, I couldn't. One compliment led to the next and I eventually found out that I wasn't as strong as I thought.

While the affair lasted a short time, the repercussions reverberated. From that day on, it seemed I would attract only married men. I could not draw single men, until I confessed my sin before God and broke contact with "Thomas".

While I had already physically and situationally cut myself off from *"Thomas"*, his spirit still lingered with me because we had become "one" through our sexual encounters.

"For as it is written, 'The two will become one flesh." **(I Corinthians 6:16**, ESV).

This is why no single man would even give me the time of day because I was already spiritually identified as "married."

SUDDENLY *Single* WIDOW'S EDITION

* * *

Once I confessed to God my sin and asked Him to divorce "Thomas" from my spirit and me from his, only then would single men once again become attracted to me. In addition, I asked God to heal me from what was lacking internally which caused me to enter such a situation. It was only then that single men would become attracted to me again.

As I began to prepare myself to be a trustworthy wife, Holy Spirit prompted me to go on a fast and get delivered from all previous lovers, "baby daddies," and even "fantasy" lovers, as these all had created soul ties.

I know that some will argue that there is no such thing as a "soul tie"; however, when you define the words separately, **soul** means "*the immaterial essence, animating principle, or actuating cause of an individual life*" (Merriam-Webster, 2022). The soul consists of the mind, the will, and the emotions. "**Tie**" in its transitive form means "*to fasten, attach; to connect, to place or establish in a relationship*" (2022). Through intimacy, *my mind, will, and emotions* became "fastened" with that of previous relationships.

I needed to be free so that my future husband would not have to compete with the spirits of any former lovers. This also meant getting rid of every picture and gifts ex-boyfriends gave me. I had to make a clean break of everything that attached me to my past, including finding a new church home far from my temptation. In my obedience, God would reveal who my future husband would be.

The Great Revelation

One Sunday at my new church, the Pastor got up and announced that he felt "led" to have all the members pray on their knees at the altar. This act was new as normally we'd stand to pray wherever we were seated in the sanctuary.

As I walked up front and began to kneel, Steve rushed from his seat in the pulpit to hand me his suit jacket to cover up.

I thought, "Now, my dress is not THAT short that he has to come running with this big ol' jacket!"

Steve was 6'2 and 224 lbs of "sheer" man, so his jacket draped over my petite frame. As I was wrapping his suit coat around me, which was still warm from his body heat, I heard the Holy Spirit whisper, "He's your covering."

I gasped.

This same *new guy* Steve, the Pastor's nephew, from earlier with whom, I had developed a *platonic* relationship.

SUDDENLY *Single* WIDOW'S EDITION

* * *

Steve was divorced a year and a half before we met. As his friend, I would often sign him up for Christian singles conferences so that he would get out and meet new people. My girls loved him. Little did I know God was assigning him to my life as my husband.

* * *

Once again, I didn't say anything to anyone about this newfound revelation. I learned that for some things, you must remain silent until after it comes to pass. Also, we would have been dangerous to each other in that particular season of life, as we were both still healing.

Yet, it didn't stop Steve and me from developing a healthy friendship. I was secretly attracted to Steve. He was "tall, dark & handsome."

However, what drew me most to him was his kindness. He was a big man with a barreling baritone voice and the heart of a teddy bear.

He was from Joiner, Arkansas where he learned hospitality and good values. Steve knew how to hunt, fish, cook, bake, clean, and protect. He adored my girls and would often speak kindly to them.

On a few occasions, Steve invited us to his home for dinner. Steve kept his home immaculately clean. At his home, Steve always kept an extra place set at his table, which he believed would be the spot for his future wife. Since I had no clue at the time that she would be me, when we did join him for dinner, I would leave that spot open in respect of his faith.

On a few occasions, Steve invited us to his home for dinner. Steve kept his home immaculately clean. At his home, Steve always kept an extra place set at his table, which he believed would be the spot for his future wife. Since I had no clue at the time that she would be me, when we did join him for dinner, I would leave that spot open in respect of his faith.

In His providence, God knew that I was exactly what & who Steve needed and vice versa. A few months would pass before Steve would finally get the revelation.

Our Relationship Takes A Turn

One day, Steve called and asked me to go to dinner with him.

This was our first date.

Unbeknownst to me then, he had already contacted my parents asking if they'd watch my girls as he wanted to do something special for me. I put on the cutest, form-flattering dress I found in my closet. It was slate gray and paired nicely with my sharp, black stilettos. It

SUDDENLY *Single* WIDOW'S EDITION

was my favorite dress. Later, I would discover it was his too, as he loved seeing me in it.

I put on my make-up and perfume and drove to meet Steve at the restaurant. We had agreed that we would meet at the location. He came in dressed sharply, pants perfectly creased, and shoes shined. He told me that I looked beautiful. While I knew that we were just two friends going to dinner, I noticed that Steve was acting differently.

As we ate and shared a few laughs, Steve leaned in and said, "You know that I've been praying and believing God for a wife for some time now. I was looking for all these particular qualities in a wife. However, it finally dawned on me that I see in you everything I was looking for."

I almost choked.

I was not expecting to hear that. I didn't know what I was hoping to hear, but it sure wasn't that!

As my face lit up from blushing, he reached across the table and grabbed my hand. He told me he wanted to take our friendship to the next level

I had no words.

Once again, my emotions gripped me. I didn't know what to say. Steve was so handsome with his big, beautiful brown eyes and solid and massive hands that were large enough to cover both of mine. I loved those hands. They were the epitome of his masculinity and strength.

Those vast hands knew how to hold and cuddle my face to bring my lips to his. They also knew how to work, as Steve had a strong work ethic. He wasn't afraid to work, often rising hours early to prepare for his day. Steve was a very dependable and trustworthy leader at his job. He never used his hands to harm me or my girls.

As we left the restaurant, Steve walked me to my car and gave me a gentle kiss on the lips. I slid down in my car seat in bliss. Of course, it was after he walked away. I couldn't let him see that he "*melted me down*" like that! As I drove home, I replayed every detail of our date in my mind and shrieked with joy.

* * *

Steve popped the question a month after our date.

However, we were going through a slight, rough patch then, and I wasn't convinced that his proposal was sincere. I needed time to process and think about what I needed. When I weighed the pros and cons of our courtship, received counseling and took the time to talk to God about everything, I knew what my decision would be.

SUDDENLY *Single* WIDOW'S EDITION

* * *

The next day at church, I walked up to Steve after the service. Steve was delighted for me to talk with him.

After our greetings, I told him, "You know what you were going to ask me last night? You can try asking me again."

Steve's face lit up.

"Will you marry me?" he asked.

"Yes, I will," I responded.

Steve laughed loudly in his boisterous voice stirring the other congregants who were still standing around talking.

"Hey, everyone! I just asked Jan to marry me, and she said 'Yes!'"

Everyone went wild, congratulating us. The deacon said, "Wait a minute! We must do this right! Grab a chair. Jan, come up front and sit in this chair. Steve, ask her again!"

So, Steve and I went to the front of the church, and while I sat in the chair with everyone surrounding us, he dropped down on one knee (no ring in sight) and asked me to marry him. He began to share how I had been a blessing to him in friendship and how he couldn't think of anyone better to have as a partner. He then asked me to be his wife

Once again, I said 'yes.'

He leaned in and we shared a brief kiss so steamy, that the other members began fanning.

I couldn't believe it.

I was getting ready to become Mrs. Mitchell.

Steve and I planned our wedding for September of that same year. However, knowing we were engaged triggered the temptation to become intimate before the wedding. As Christians, we endeavored to live an abstinent life until marriage. However, we were both incredibly tempted and made a few "close calls," which prompted us to move the wedding date up sooner.

We wanted to be honorable in our intentions towards one another, especially with both of us working in ministry. It was work.

So, we moved our date to June 18, 2011, exactly two weeks after Steve had proposed. I didn't know it then, but Steve had asked my Dad's permission to take my hand in marriage. I love "old-fashioned" chivalry. I bought my dress and had my hair styled the night before the wedding. One of the members and her husband graciously decorated the church for us.

SUDDENLY *Single* WIDOW'S EDITION

We stayed in a fabulous hotel, a gift from our church leadership. For our first year anniversary, we had a second honeymoon in Cancun, Mexico. It was an all-expenses paid trip that I had won through my job.

Beautiful story, right?

Not a perfect one, but a beautiful one. Yet, one that abruptly ended five and half years later as Steve would pass away from hospital-acquired sepsis.

No bride or groom walks down the aisle expecting to have to bury their spouse. Sure, we quote the traditional wedding vows, "in sickness and health, for better or for worse, for richer or for poorer, until death do us part."

However, we don't expect death to come *SUDDENLY!*

Death is a cruel, unfair reality of living. It causes much pain, fear, and plenty of questions, like:

"Why did this happen to me?"

"Where is God?"

"Why didn't God heal my spouse?"

"Did I do everything I could have to prevent my loved one's death?"

"Was I a good spouse to them?"

Jan Mitchell

"Did they truly know how much I loved them?"

And on and on, the questions flow.

We might have even been angry with our spouses at the time of their death.

As time moves forward after the death of our beloved, we may begin to wonder how we can start to heal and process this new journey. We may have questions about how we begin to move forward when it feels like some days our feet are stuck in quicksand.

We pick up one foot to move forward, to find out it's too painful. We're heavy. Grief is heavy, and we feel like we're sinking. Yet, there is hope, joy, and new LIFE on the other side of our pain.

But how do we get from here to there?

CHAPTER II:

Grief Is Not

Linear Nor Is It A Life Sentence

I recall the first few hours, days, and weeks after Steve's passing. There were some very rough days when it seemed that I would not stop crying.

Then there were days I'd feel just fine. The next moment it would feel as if I had not even been married. It was like everything about Steve and our marriage was merely a fairytale or dream that never existed. It was weird. And there were days when I just felt numb.

There were days that I was fearful of feeling the pain. I thought that if I allowed myself to feel the intensity of the sadness, it would consume me. This fear led me to blow off the feelings of grief as long as I could. I did this by keeping myself uber-busy with different activities.

Some of you can relate.

First, you may have never been a widow or widower. Be gracious to yourself. This experience is a unique journey for you.

You lost the love of your life—the one with whom you expected to share many decades and eternity. For younger widows and widowers, you didn't expect to lose your spouse so young.

That's hard.

SUDDENLY *Single* **WIDOW'S EDITION**

Take your time and heal properly. Seek a healthy support system that can minister to your particular needs as a young widow/er. Also, know that becoming a widow is not an inherently shameful thing. You're not destined to live forever with the proverbial "dark cloud" hovering over your head.

You may also find that just because you know other widow(er)s in your life doesn't automatically mean they'll be your best bud. I've learned that most times, they can't be there for you because either they're still processing their grief (no matter how long a time it's been) or because they are afraid of reopening those wounds.

They may have also healed through their journey and no longer want to revisit that season. We must be willing to extend grace to them as well as we would expect for ourselves. Often, we will find ourselves on this journey alone, and we must be willing to do the work to rebuild a life for ourselves.

Perspectives On Grief

According to the Mayo Clinic, grief is a "strong, sometimes overwhelming emotion for people, regardless of whether their sadness stems from the loss of a loved one or from a terminal diagnosis they or someone they love have received" (mayoclinic.org, 2016).

There are five known stages of grief:

1. Denial
2. Anger
3. Bargaining
4. Depression
5. Acceptance

However, recent studies have added two more stages of grief:

6. Disbelief and Shock
7. Guilt and pain

(gatewaycounseling.com)

Unfortunately, as these lists suggest, grief does not always hit us in perfect or linear order. Grief often hits you when you least expect it. It could also start to occur before the person dies.

This is a type of grief called "anticipatory grief."

Anticipatory grief is grief that comes *before* the passing of a spouse or loved one. This form of grief is often linked to someone who has suffered a long-standing illness, such as cancer, HIV, or any other terminal ailment.

This style of grief sometimes can seem a little less tense than the grief that comes with a sudden loss.

SUDDENLY *Single* WIDOW'S EDITION

This is because the caregiver has already experienced a level of grief during the spouse's illness.

Anticipatory grief is the type of grief that I experienced with Steve. While Steve's death was unexpected, I still grieved his many nights in the hospital away from the girls and me. I lamented his absence even though I would travel to the hospital daily to visit him. *The hospital was not home.* I grieved the absence of his barreling laugh. After his spinal cord injury, Steve experienced severe respiratory issues, which impacted his ability to laugh fully as he once had.

I grieved while Steve was still alive.

For some time, he could not breathe on his own. Therefore, he could not laugh or speak with any of us. Steve flatlined four times during the first 30 days of his hospitalization, which required him to be put on a ventilator and trach for life support. When God blessed Steve to be weaned off both apparatuses, he still couldn't laugh as fully as before.

The spinal cord injury he sustained paralyzed him from the inside out, which meant that his diaphragm muscles and other internal organs were also impacted.

When most think of anticipatory grief, they often think we're saying it's "easier" to process than a sudden death. No, it's not. Death is still a blow to the survivor, whether sudden or expected. Please don't stress yourself trying to compare your grief journey to another's. Regardless of the circumstances that led to the death, we all need and desire compassion and time.

Take, for instance, the loss of many lives during the global COVID-19 pandemic of 2019-2022. Hundreds of thousands of souls worldwide died due to a horrific virus still making subtle waves, despite new vaccinations and research.

Before many of these dear ones passed, they suffered from the virus for some time, whether short or long. Families were praying, hoping, and sending positive thoughts and vibes in anticipation of their loved one recovering from the virus. Yet, death met them.

As many watched the daily decline of their loved one and therefore adjusted to "expect" death, dare we judge their grief any less painful than the one who kissed their loved one goodbye that morning, only to receive tragic news later that day? What about the loved one whose long-term, deep depression led to suicide? Death is still death.

And it's a sucky blow.

We must be careful not to judge another's grief experience. Just as no one human is the same,

SUDDENLY *Single* WIDOW'S EDITION

including identical twins, no one's grief journey will look the same. Even though we all may have lost a spouse and have very *similar* stories of how our loved one passed, our experience is still unique. We must learn to be compassionate with others as well as ourselves during our season of grief.

While grieving Steve's death, I found that my first feeling after he took his last breath in front of me was shock and *relief*. The relief came from knowing that the anticipated wait was over.

Four days before Steve passed, the doctor had informed us that he had become septic by way of Cdiff-affected stool which had leaked into an unbandaged stage IV bedsore. This led to the Cdiff tainting Steve's bloodstream.

Those last four days were a complete HELL watching Steve slowly decline each day. We had chosen palliative care to provide comfort care for him versus putting him back on ventilation.

After Steve had been weaned from the vent the first time, he complained of a persistent sore throat. Having the tube inserted previously had been very painful for him. He nor I wanted him to experience that level of trauma again.

.

Jan Mitchell

* * *

Steve was placed on a morphine drip and provided ice chips to keep his mouth and lips moist during the dying process. Because Steve's body had begun to shut down, he was no longer permitted to eat any foods due to the fear of asphyxiation. The muscles in his throat had started to relax, which caused a medical concern that he might choke and suffocate to death from solid food intake.

Watching Steve go through this process was sheer torment as Steve loved to eat. To hear him state that he was hungry, with the small strength he could muster to even speak each day was heartbreaking.

In addition to the ice chips, Steve was also put on a liquid diet which was issued through a feeding tube; which eased concerns. Steve's death relieved him because he no longer had to suffer.

> *I wish that the healthcare sector would develop a better process to aid the dying as well as support their families when it seems as if the dying is being starved to death.*

SUDDENLY *Single* WIDOW'S EDITION

* * *

One thing that I learned while going through the various stages of grief is that you ***cannot*** do it alone.

I wasn't the only one grieving. My daughters were also grieving the loss of their Dad. My family, especially my dad, grieved Steve.

Steve had been an instrumental father figure in the lives of my two oldest daughters who were not biologically his.

However, Steve never made a distinction between them and his biological daughters. I knew that I could not process my grief and help my daughters manage theirs on my own. I went on the hunt for a grief group that would assist us in our new journey.

* * *

I found the search for a grief group for widows a bit difficult as most of the classes were held in the middle of the work week in the early mornings or around lunch time. I still worked a job and I still had young children to raise. Attending the classes was unrealistic for my schedule as a single mom.

In addition to the conflict with the grief group schedule, I also found that most of the widows and widowers in the class seemed to be sixty-five years of age and older. These beautiful individuals had had decades of memories with their spouses and were retired. Their children were grown and had their own families.

While their grief was just as precious as mine, I didn't have the years with Steve to be able to relate to the stories of the others in the room. It was an awkward experience to walk into those grief groups and be the youngest person in the room. I was thirty-eight years old at the time of Steve's passing.

After much searching and reaching out to the palliative care team that assisted me with Steve, I discovered Brooke's Place. It is a fantastic facility dedicated to helping children process grief through various means of play and psycho (talk) therapy in both group and individual settings.

Brooke's Place also had a separate class for the parents who were also processing grief or helping their children to cope. This class proved beneficial to my schedule as it was held in the evenings, and they always served fresh, hot pizza, cookies, and drinks to the families before we would separate into our classes. These nights meant that I had a night off from cooking!

The therapy proved to be an excellent benefit for my children and me as it equipped us with the skills, tools, and camaraderie to process our grief.

SUDDENLY *Single* WIDOW'S EDITION

On those Tuesday evenings at Brooke's Place, I could share and listen to the others in the adult group who had experienced a loss. The unique thing about the class was that not all were grieving the loss of a spouse. Everyone had a special reason as to why they were there.

We had a great facilitator and group. We built friendships with one another, provided advice to one another, and ate and cried with each other. We built a solid camaraderie amongst ourselves. In this room, we were allowed to express our feelings freely without judgment. It was everything we all needed.

* * *

I also chose to continue to meet with our marriage counselor.
Steve and I had met her early in our marriage. She had proven to be very instrumental in me and Steve's relationship. "Roxanne" provided us with the tools we needed to learn how to navigate our blended family with all its usual challenges.

Continuing to meet with her even after Steve's passing provides comfort since she knew Steve so well and is a familiar voice of comfort and reason.

JAN MITCHELL

Abnormal Grief

Many times, in this grief journey, you will hear many tell you that no one can put a time limit on your grief. This is true as grief is a personal journey that we all will travel at some time in our lives.

We will lose friends, family, and other loved ones. However, the death of a spouse is especially grievous, as you lose your partner, along with the dreams and plans you had anticipated together.

Again, we accept that death is a natural part of the living experience and grief takes time to process. However, there is such a thing called "abnormal grief" or "complicated grief."

As aforementioned, "normal" grief traditionally has five stages. According to The American Journal of Psychotherapy, normal grief progresses from acute to integrated grief, which is where we must accept the loss.

This progression manifests through the decreased intensity of mental suffering when you remember your loved one and have recommitted to life.

*Kendler, Myers, & Zisook, 2008; Zisook & Kendler, 2007; Zisook, Paulus, Shuchter, & Judd, 1997; Zisook, Schneider, & Shuchter, 1990; Zisook & Shear, 2009; Zisook, Shear, & Kendler, 2007; Zisook & Shuchter, 1991b)

SUDDENLY *Single* WIDOW'S EDITION

However, 'abnormal grief' or it's medical term, 'complicated grief,' persists and typically shows in symptoms such as **sleep disturbance** (Germain, Caroff, Buysse, & Shear, 2005; Hardison, Neimeyer, & Lichstein, 2005; McDermott et al., 1997), *social-professional dysfunction* (Boelen & Prigerson, 2007; Simon et al., 2005; Simon et al., 2007), *suicidal ideas and behaviors* (Latham & Prigerson, 2004; Szanto et al., 2006), and **higher general mortality** (Helsing & Szklo, 1981; Stroebe, Schut & Stroebe, 2007).

If you notice the latter symptoms overtaking you, please seek professional help as soon as possible. Yes, I believe in the power of prayer, but I also know that God uses professional & credentialed people to help us. Seeking professional help is not an indication of a lack of faith. Instead, it can be proof of your faith

"Faith without works is dead." **(James 2:17**, KJV).

DISCLAIMER: *I do not claim to be a physician, therapist, or counselor. Please seek counsel from a licensed professional as needed.*

---

* * *

What kept me from sinking into abnormal grief, was having a healthy support system, professional counseling, and my faith, although it was severely, but not *permanently*, shaken.

Yes, I went through a brief stint where I struggled in my faith after Steve's passing. It was hard to imagine why God would allow such a thing to happen.

Both my biological and church families assisted me in staying grounded during my grieving process, but they could & would not always be there. Different ones would offer to come by my home and assist with cooking, cleaning, and watching my children while I rested.

While I was grateful for the many offers, I was very protective and selective of whom I allowed in my space. It is vital that when you are choosing your "core" people to be available during your grief, you select trustworthy, dependable, and safe people. Grief is enough to deal with. You do not need any added drama trying to appease others.

However, I want to caution that while loved ones are there for us in our vulnerable times, they will not or cannot always be there. Please do not hold that against them, as they must move forward with their lives. It is essential during grief that you take care of yourself. Sometimes, that means allowing others to assist you, but know that it may not last always.

SUDDENLY *Single* WIDOW'S EDITION

Prolonged or complicated grief can also occur because we do not have or take the time to grieve appropriately due to constant, ongoing responsibilities, such as raising children, working a job, or ministry.

Saying "NO" to those things that are not priorities this season is imperative. This includes telling yourself "No" to the "superman" or "superwoman" syndrome. It's okay to ask for help. Delegate duties. It is okay to ask for assistance to help you manage some of the responsibilities you might carry.

Ask someone to babysit your children while you take time for yourself. Go to the park and have a "walk and cry." Take time and cry with your children. This was one thing that I regret that I did not do more of. I am a "closet crier," so I tend to suppress my strong emotions for a time and secluded place.

However, I found that sometimes our children are more resilient than we know and appreciate the opportunity to cry with their parents as it shows them that they are not grieving alone.

One evening, one of the girls was having a tough day, and she usually kept her door locked (yet, I have figured out how to "rig" it.) When I entered the room, she had a picture of Steve in a memory box she had made at Brooke's Place. She could barely catch her breath between gasps, "Why did he have to go?" I sat on the bed beside her and put my arm around her. I reassured her that everything would be all right.

Nevertheless, I was not entirely sure *I* believed that. As she wept, I "stayed strong" in order not to break down. My tears choked in my throat, but my stubborn pride refused to allow me to buckle as I had convinced myself that I needed to "be strong" for her at that moment.

Sound familiar?

Nevertheless, strength for her at that moment would have looked like a mother who was strong enough to cry and admit her pain so her daughter did not feel alone.

If you have younger children in school, it is good to seek grief counseling at the child's school so they may have access to a licensed professional when needed. I signed my children up as they were in a new school district where no one knew them and would not recognize their fluctuating behavioral patterns brought on by grief.

While it is true that children seem to manage grief better, keep an eye on your babies for any signs of excessive grief or depression. My daughters had grown rather fond of "their Steve," so losing him devastated them. Enrolling them in the school grief program, in addition to the outside support groups, provided extra support.

* * *

Ecclesial wisdom states, *"There is a time for everything, and a season for every activity under the heavens.... a time to weep and a time to laugh, a time to mourn and time to dance."* **(Ecclesiastes 3:1-4)**

Normal grief affords us the time and season to weep and grieve as needed.

Cry when you need to.

Studies have found that tears caused by grief, trauma, or stress carry more toxic byproducts than regular tears.

When we cry, we remove toxins from our bodies that accumulate through the build-up of stress. With the release of such toxins, crying can also elevate your mood and lowers stress (psychcentral.com, 2022), cleansing your heart and mind. Tears carry healing properties, so weep as needed.

Seven months

That is how much time passed after Steve died before I *really* cried.

Because I did not SCREAM, KICK, FAINT, OR CRY at Steve's memorial service, some questioned the validity of my love for him. However, it was LOVE for Steve that I spent seven days a week for five and a half months straight, traveling to various hospitals, rehabs, and nursing homes learning how to care for Steve after his SCI.

I spent many days cleaning his trach, feeding him, being his shoulder to cry on, and being his "voice" when he had the ventilator tube down his throat. I also was the one he trusted to train the new incoming nurses how to perform the "quad assist" technique when he needed to cough up phlegm. I was not a nurse nor held a nursing degree, but I had acquired the skill from watching the other experienced nurses who cared enough to take the time to teach me.

In many ways, I would learn to love and care for Steve on a new level in our *new normal*. I did this by God's grace while managing children, a home, a ministry, and a job. It is what you do when you genuinely love someone and are committed to your wedding vows, "in sickness and in health...til death do us part."

However, I did not permit myself to cry until later. Because I **had** to be *strong*.

Sound familiar?

SUDDENLY *Single* WIDOW'S EDITION

As quoted earlier, there is a *time* and a *season* for everything. There was a time for me to mourn Steve's absence properly. While, again, no one can dictate or tell you when to stop mourning your loved one, and that is certainly not my intention, I also have experienced that seasons do *change.*

Those of us who are blessed to live in a four seasons state (even though I am still not overly fond of snow and cold weather..ha!) , we understand the value and purpose of moving through each season.

Every season: spring, summer, fall, and winter play a significant part in the environment and land. One season helps the next and they usually last about three months each before moving into the next. Sometimes, they seem to blend right into one another, just like grief, which sometimes wants to follow us into a season ordained for peace.

May I challenge you to be willing to change with the seasons and fight the urge to feel guilty for doing so? Release the guilt of moving forward. Just because you choose to heal does not mean you have forgotten your spouse. It simply means you have decided to LIVE.

As trauma coach Venus Chandler, states, *"Healing is a choice."*

To process grief healthily and move forward into healing, we must be active participants. **Psalm 30:5** states, *"Weeping may endure for a night, but joy comes in the morning."* (KJV)

Our "joy" comes when we decide to end our mourning. Sorrow, pain, and grief were meant to only last for a season. Naturally speaking, we can ignore our morning by pulling the covers over our heads and sleeping the day away (which is not always bad; sometimes, we need the extra rest). Alternatively, we can decide to get up and see what the new day will bring. The same principle applies spiritually. We are empowered to choose to end our "night" of grieving. A promise of joy resides on the other side of *our decision* to choose to heal.

Our loved ones know how much we loved them or hated them, in some cases. There's nothing we can do to change any of that. If there was pain associated before the death, receive forgiveness for yourself. Let yourself off the hook. Release the pain and FORGIVE OTHERS!

Unforgiveness can keep us imprisoned in a season of prolonged grief.

SUDDENLY *Single* WIDOW'S EDITION

* * *

If not adequately tended to, complicated grief can become an addiction. Yes, we can become addicted to grief and brokenness as it can bring a sense of attention that helps us process and comfort ourselves during our newfound loneliness. I found myself often retelling my story of how I became a widow with any incident that came up, as it often garnered the attention, care, and comfort of new listeners.

While it achieved my momentary goal, it did not remove my deep pain. Thankfully, complicated grief can be broken by developing new habits to replace the old ones.

Be gentle with yourself in the process of change. Start with something small, such as getting up and putting a shirt on instead of remaining in your pajamas for the day. It may seem menial but getting dressed is an accomplishment in early grief.

But you can do it.

I can recall the first few days and weeks after Steve's passing. It was a chore to press myself to get up and get dressed, but I knew that I had to get up and LIVE!

Steve wouldn't want me to die just because he had. He would encourage me to LIVE!

Again, <u>no one</u> can tell you how long you should grieve. However, it is up to YOU to determine when you want to heal.

Say this with me: *"I consciously decide to heal and experience joy again. I forgive myself for any residual bitterness and guilt from the death of my spouse. I forgive those who hurt me in the wake of my grief. I receive forgiveness and grace and hope to move forward in peace. I desire and choose to heal and will not be ashamed to do so!*

CHAPTER III:

Money & Other Matters

I did not realize how many decisions and phone calls I would still need to make after the death of my spouse. Calls to the insurance companies, funeral homes, bill collectors, credit bureaus, and the list went on.

In the first few weeks of grief, I recall being advised not to make significant purchases or decisions. This is extremely important as grief impairs your ability to think correctly, negatively impacting your financial decisions.

Communication with our spouses about final arrangements and death should have occurred before their passing, whether young or old. I know that sometimes, we do not always do this. Steve and I did not communicate about death at all before his passing. We didn't talk about it because we didn't expect it.

Yes, I was aware of Steve's health condition (seizures and lupus) before marrying him, yet no young bride thinks of death coming anytime soon after marriage. When we recited our vows of "til death do us part," we were expecting to be old and gray by the time death greeted us.

SUDDENLY *Single* WIDOW'S EDITION

The day after Steve passed, I was making phone calls to the funeral home, our insurance companies, his employer, and the banks. I needed to cover his funeral expenses.

I also had to make phone calls to the credit reporting agencies: Transunion, Experian, and Equifax. After the death of a loved one, you must contact each agency and provide an original copy of the death certificate. You will want to make sure that you keep multiple copies of the original death certificate for business purposes; copying these documents will help protect the deceased's identity from theft.

Cover them in their death as you did while they were living.

Call the utility companies and provide them with a death certificate, as this will also stop treacherous relatives or other thieves from using your deceased loved one's identity.

You can avoid this by contacting utility companies and getting the death certificate in their hands. If your health insurance company did not ultimately pay these bills off, any medical bills that may have accumulated from long-term stays or treatments, may be written off or forgiven. Contact the hospital or care facility as soon as possible. It's best to have a trusted friend or family member to assist you in these matters. Let the healthcare facility know of the departure of your loved one.

Most hospitals have charities and assistance programs that either cover 50%, if not all, of the debt or it can be written off. You may also consider consulting with a lawyer, as they can advise what other debts can be eliminated. Check for pro bono lawyer services in your local area to assist you in these matters.

Finances And Money

You cannot rely on everyone to help you with your finances, as people can become nosey. They want to know what you have or what you are getting. You don't need everyone in your affairs. All you need is a small, trustworthy support team who can help you through the process. That may include a lawyer, your banker, and one trusted family member or friend. That's it. When you have a blended family with minor children, such as I did, seek guidance regarding finances.

Per IRS rules, surviving dependents are eligible to receive social security benefits until they are 18 or disabled. If you and your loved one share a joint bank account, you will want to notify your bankers or brokers so that the bank can allocate the funds. If you carried individual or separate accounts, providing a copy of your original marriage certificate, death certificate, and photo ID should be sufficient to transfer any funds. Check with your bank to confirm what documentation you will need.

SUDDENLY *Single* WIDOW'S EDITION

You will also need to revisit and re-establish (or establish, if this is your first time) a budget that will be conducive to losing the additional working income from the deceased. Financial adjustments will need to be made so that you can live comfortably after the death of your spouse, especially if you still have minor children living in your home.

Adopt the use of coupons and cash envelopes so that you are aware of what you are spending versus having to use a credit card or debit card to swipe for purchases. Carrying cash causes us to be aware of what we're spending.

I had to re-establish a budget based on the loss of income and new living conditions that I found myself in.

Again, be mindful of how you're spending or ask for help, so you don't do as I did. I overspent on a vehicle after Steve's passing. It was a certified vehicle, a few years old, with one owner and under 35k miles. I ended up paying more than the car's worth and with cash. Had I listened to wisdom and avoided making this purchase during grief, I would have saved myself thousands of dollars.

To my credit, I am not the "average" female car shopper, as I usually do my due diligence in researching (Carfax, Kelley Blue Book, etc.), recruiting my male family members for guidance, and test-driving a vehicle. However, due to my vulnerable state, I overpaid.

Thankfully, I was able to recoup some losses, but it took me a while to stop grieving the loss of the original thousands I could have saved. Yet, there are no regrets, only experience and a hard, but good lesson learned.

In addition to becoming a widow, I also learned that I could carry my spouse on my taxes for two years per the IRS and receive the benefits of a joint tax return.

You would file as a "qualifying widow or widower" (www.irs.gov). This knowledge helps provide additional income during tax season when it is most needed.

And again, if you have younger children, remember to sign them up for survivors' benefits which both dependent biological and stepchildren under 18 can receive.

CHAPTER IV:

Surviving The Firsts

Jan Mitchell

The "firsts" are always met with a level of anxiety.

We don't know how we will feel when the first wedding anniversary, birthday or any of the major holidays rolls around and our spouse is no longer there. We hold our breath in anticipation of how we "think" we may feel or react on that day.

I have heard various stories from other widows/ers who expected to feel complete devastation when that "first" came around and it was the total opposite. They felt peace. Of course, others reported feeling completely out of control and spent their day in tears and emotional meltdowns.

However, be mindful of exhaling and being gentle with your experience. Your experience is unique to *you*.

* * *

I recall my first Thanksgiving and Christmas without Steve. It was a bit surreal, as I purchased a new home six months after his passing. I did not want to stay in the same place where Steve had suffered his injury and where we had shared so many memories. I still had a closetful of his clothes which I packed up to give away, yet the smell of his cologne seemed embedded in every place in the house. The girls and I needed a fresh start—a new change.

SUDDENLY *Single* WIDOW'S EDITION

That first Christmas, I purchased the most giant tree I could find and allowed the girls to decorate it as they saw fit. One of my daughters put a picture of Steve on one of the branches. When she did this, it brought tears to my eyes as I knew that Steve would have loved to have celebrated with us in our new home.

Yet, I had to become creative as this holiday could not be like all the others before. Because it wasn't. Steve wasn't there.

Creativity looked like inviting family over and having a giant slumber party. I don't mind spending time with family, but I prefer a quiet house when it's time to rest. It's my ambivert personality.

So, inviting family over to spend the night was out of my comfort zone. However, it was a lot of fun and made the holidays easier. The girls were excited. You can either create a new tradition with your family or keep the one you already had. I heard one widow state that she still labels Christmas gifts with "From Dad & Mom", as they're still family, regardless of Dad's transition. I love that! You could begin something that you believe would honor the memory of your loved one. Your new practice can be gentle and exciting but use it to realign your hearts and mind with peace and love.

Jan Mitchell

A New Normal: Owning A Home Alone

Speaking of houses, owning a home without a spouse, especially without a husband, can be very difficult. This is a first for many. You don't realize how much your spouse contributed to the upkeep of the household until after they are no longer there. Even the seemingly minor things, such as managing pesky spiders that might want to build their web home in the corner of your ceiling, can be intimidating.

Steve was from the country, so catching mice, laying mice traps, and killing spiders, wasps and the like was nothing to him. Thankfully, I only had one scare of a field mouse entering my house through the garage. I allowed my older girls and Mom to take care of the problem.

Haha!

They had more guts than I did I had to learn how to cut grass and trim hedges until I found a reasonably priced lawn company. However, in the fragile monetary state most widows and widowers find themselves in, I encourage learning to maintain these things themselves or utilize your children's assistance.

SUDDENLY *Single* WIDOW'S EDITION

My girls loved working in the yard with me; we found it very therapeutic.

The upkeep of a home without a spouse may be overwhelming. This is a "first" for many widows/ers. Carpets need to be cleaned; tile needs to be restored; the roof starts to leak, and on and on the list goes. cleaned, tile needs to be restored, the roof starts to leak, and on and on the list goes.

If you can afford to have someone do these things make the connection. I suggest shopping around for a few quotes so that you may be able to pay for all jobs. Becoming a widow(er) decreases our finances, so we must take extra caution in how we spend, especially if we are single parents.

If you happen to attend a church or another nonprofit organization, support entrepreneurs who may have small maintenance businesses. Sometimes, you can find the best help for the least price right within your circle. Utilize those connections and support local small business owners.

I know it's hard when you were used to being able to say, "Hey babe, this is broken," and have it "magically" fixed by the end of the day. Home maintenance is tough enough for two, let alone one person!

Since Steve passed, I've learned to unclog a backed-up sink from underneath, replace shower heads, and do many other household chores. I'm grateful for YouTube university! I am proud of my ability to have learned something new, though I wouldn't say I liked the reason why I had to learn.

But, the pride I felt encouraged my spirits and reassured me that I could handle the task, which meant I could handle other things.

Downsizing may be something to consider if your children are grown and living independently. If taking care of your home and meeting your mortgage is now difficult due to the loss of your spouse's income, downsizing may prove beneficial. In addition, if you and your spouse still owed vehicle payments, consider trading either one or both cars in This can help you save on auto repairs if your cars are older than five years. New cars come with a warranty to cover expensive repair costs.

The First Anniversary

First-year wedding anniversaries can be excruciating after the death of a spouse. My "first" wedding anniversary without Steve came just four months after his passing. Steve passed February 2017. Our wedding anniversary was in June.

For that first anniversary, I took that weekend off from work, and while the kids were still in school, I drove to one of my favorite parks in the city. I loved this park

SUDDENLY *Single* WIDOW'S EDITION

because it had a lovely walking and hiking trail and a botanical garden.

Steve and I visited this park a few times before with the girls. I went to the park early that morning when I knew there wouldn't be many people. I took my earbuds and plugged into worship music. I also took a notepad and pen with me while visiting the garden. There, I would sit down and write out my angry & painful thoughts. It was one of the ways that I would use to "release" the pain and the bitterness from my heart. I didn't hold anything back in that letter, even allowing myself to slip in a few profanities:

Dear Such-and-Such, I am so angry with you right now. Why did you act the way that you did? Why would you believe that I was out to harm Steve when all I tried to do was show him love? We could have had a grand celebration of life for Steve had you communicated with me."

And on and on, my letter went.

* * *

According to the American Psychological Association, writing strengthens the immune system and the mind, which helps people manage and learn from their negative experiences (**www.apa.org, 2022**).

After writing the letter, I wept. I wept for Steve. I wept for the gaping hole I felt in my soul and heart. I cried out of frustration towards my in-laws. I wept because while listening to gospel worship songs, I wasn't quite sure how I felt about God. I still loved Him, but I was angry with Him. I felt like God was punishing me and that I was only getting what I deserved for the past sins that I had committed.

Yet, I felt terrible because I was blaming Him. I already knew what He had told me about taking Steve.

God didn't leave me "blindsided."

Even as I type, I pause and reflect on how far I've come from that first anniversary to where I am now. In that moment of pain, I couldn't envision myself <u>ever</u> feeling peace again.

I was a bundle of emotions that day.

After taking a few deep breaths, I got up and began to move forward with my nature walk. When I got home that evening, I cooked Steve's favorite meal for me and the girls

That night, I just couldn't stop staring at our wedding pictures. The more I looked at his handsome face in

SUDDENLY *Single* WIDOW'S EDITION

those pictures, the more I became frustrated with him not being there.

Especially at that moment.

I needed my man there with me to hold me. To caress and kiss me. To make love to me. Dang, I missed his fine, goofy self!

The First Gravesite Visit

I recall another significant first for me: visiting Steve's grave in Arkansas. I rode with my sibling and Mom. Remember from my first book, "*Suddenly Single: Surviving the Demise of Your Relationship,*" I stated how I did not attend Steve's funeral due to all the drama that had taken place.

The potential for things to turn volatile was a reality. I chose to protect me and my girls' peace by not attending. However, I planned a beautiful memorial and worship service, which I knew Steve would be proud of as he was a "praiser." Steve loved to praise the Lord.

As I had not planned a funeral before, I didn't realize that it takes several months for the ground to settle after a grave is covered. This meant that the final headstone had not yet been placed, which initially made it hard to locate his plot. However, a small marker on the ground with Steve's name listed identified his spot.

Steve was buried in a small church cemetery where his mother once attended. Once we found his plot, we noticed weeds growing around the site, so we drove to the closest local store to buy gardening tools and trash bags.

My Mom, sister, and I began to clean up Steve's spot. As we began to pull up the weeds and lay fresh flowers, I felt a sudden and overwhelming urge to keep digging until I unearthed Steve's casket. I wanted to pull him out of there and bring him back home ALIVE to Indianapolis with me!

The sudden &overwhelming surge of emotions surprised me. However, God has a sense of humor and knows when to employ it because just as suddenly as I had begun to be overwhelmed, Holy Spirit reminded me that I was in Arkansas. Arkansas has snakes! This thought brought me back to reality as I didn't want to dig up a snake while tidying up Steve's grave!

There would have been two bodies at the grave if that had happened!

Navigating the "firsts" after the death of your spouse is not easy. I won't pretend it is nor minimize how you might experience your "firsts ." Everyone's journey is their own. The patterns of death are challenging every time, but they help us grow if we seek them.

Allow yourself to feel what you feel at that moment

Then choose to heal.

CHAPTER V:

Drama & Forgiveness

I hate that this even happens. Isn't it enough that you've already gone through the loss of your spouse? Who wants to deal with drama amid grief?

However, we know it happens. My situation was no different. I've come to learn that death brings out the worst in people. Better yet, death reveals what was already in a person's heart.

Drama tends to show up when there is long-held bitterness, jealousy, and other forms of strife between individuals. *"The patterns of death are challenging every time, but they help us grow if we seek them."*

Forgiveness is a way to grow through and past the challenges of death. Berkley University's publication, "Greater Good Magazine," defines forgiveness as "*a conscious, deliberate decision to release feelings of resentment or vengeance toward a person or group who has harmed you, regardless of whether they deserve it*" (2022).

Unforgiveness is a state of emotional and mental distress resulting from a delayed response in forgiving the offender. It is characterized by indignation, bitterness, and a demand for punishment or restitution **(Rowett, A., 2022)**.

Unforgiveness creates a domino effect that negatively impacts us holistically: emotionally, physically, spiritually, and may even impact us financially. Suddenly, everything and everyone in our path begs

---

Offense and unforgiveness leaves us broken spiritually and emotionally. But it also chains us to the offender in our conscious and hearts.

---

our mercy as our children, family, and friends are often the receivers of our bitterness. We become unable to see the good in anyone and we begin to become suspicious of everyone's motives. We overspend on new purchases to appear "impressive" to our enemies. Offense and unforgiveness leave us broken spiritually and emotionally.

The saying goes, *"Hating someone is like drinking poison and expecting the other person to die from it."*

In other words, unforgiveness slowly kills us. Research has even shown that many illnesses can result from harboring unforgiveness. Clara Naum states, "It's not that unforgiveness causes cancer. It's that the suppression of anger, resentment, and grief disrupts the normal operation of our bodies. These disruptions lead to weakened immune system responses, and it's this weakened immune system that opens the door to illnesses and diseases" (claranaum.com).

But that does not have to be our fate. It's up to us to choose to forgive.

False Accusations

I had a decent relationship with my in-laws. There was one who was not thrilled about me and Steve's relationship

In the beginning, there were only well wishes. But as the months progressed and her marriage began to dissolve, she became very bitter and envious of what Steve and I shared. Her actions showed up a few times after our marriage when we interacted with her.

We would see the apparent discord, but continued to show kindness and forgiveness towards her.

Like most, I struggle with individuals who underhandedly and deceptively work to create unrest in others' lives. I knew she was jealous; however, I did not find out how much so until Steve suffered his injury.

SUDDENLY *Single* WIDOW'S EDITION

She began to spread rumors to other family members that Steve's injury was due to my attempt to murder him. Her false accusation was that Steve caught me with another man, and because of the confrontation, I shoved Steve down a flight of stairs.

The story was incredulously hilarious to me when I heard it! We didn't have stairs in our home. At that time, we lived in an apartment on the ground level. She knew this as she had visited once. I thought the story was hilarious and laughed until my belly hurt when I was confronted with the story.

The laugh was just what I needed during the stress of Steve's hospitalization. When false rumors and lies come up against you, laugh! When anxiety and grief attempt to overwhelm and overtake you, laugh! Grab a comedy movie or attend a live show and laugh!

Laughter or a merry heart is healing like medicine. I told the individual who shared the story with me, "She could have come to me, and I would have come up with a better story than that. I must call Blair Underwood and tell him it's over between us!"

While I had sincerely laughed and the stress was momentarily relieved, an hour later, when she stepped into the hospital waiting room, rage hit me. Every fiber of my being told me to go and "drag" her along the hospital floors.

Yet, I was surrounded by a praying mother, loving and supportive relatives, and a church family who had my back. Also, as a Christian, I have the indwelling Comforter. I may not always cooperate with Him, but His love restrains me. His love doesn't make me foolish or a doormat, but He gives me wisdom through His word on handling difficult situations.

With tensions high due to the level of injury that Steve had sustained, some of the family members with who I thought I had a good relationship began to believe the instigator. Those same loved ones attempted to "steal" Steve's body from the mortuary I had requested to perform Steve's final arrangements. Thankfully, the staff caught and stopped this act amidst many threats made to them by others.

All this drama could have been prevented by proper communication.

I held anger, bitterness, hate, and resentment toward those who had behaved unfairly and unjustly toward me. It was already enough to experience the pain of losing my spouse. Yet, every day of the five and half months that Steve remained in various hospitals and rehab facilities, I went through daily battles with the family. And then, to top it off, they wanted to pull this foolishness.

I felt conflicted. One part of me felt justified in my anger, but the other part was grieved because they were still family. I wanted our children to know them for their sake and Steve's because I knew he would like that. He was a family man. However, this did not mean exposing my children to unhealthy individuals because they were family.

As a parent, you are responsible for your child's well-being, not only physically but psychologically. I know the saying goes that "blood is thicker than water," and it is. But when there's an unhealthy situation involved with "blood," then you must decide what is in the best interest of the child. If the offender begins to show a pattern of change, pray and ask God if and when it's appropriate to reconcile.

Notice that I said "reconcile," not forgive. Forgiveness and reconciliation are two separate transactions. You can forgive someone and not necessarily need to reconcile, especially if they have a track history of being unsafe.

The definition of reconciling means, "To restore friendly relations between; to cause to co-exist in harmony; make or show to be compatible or to make someone accept a disagreeable or unwelcome thing." (www.merriamwebster.com, 2022) Just as it takes deciding to heal, it also requires the same to forgive.

Forgiveness is not a feeling: It's a decision.

Choosing Forgiveness

Forgiveness is an essential part of healing from grief. When we refuse to forgive, whether it's the late spouse we argued with because they wouldn't listen to our wise advice concerning their health or other matters, or your anger has waxed hot against the family troublemakers, we hold ourselves in a past state of existence.

What do I mean by that?

Unforgiveness locks you both naturally and spiritually in a prison of the past, mentally, emotionally, and psychologically. We may look like we're moving forward and doing well, but you can only "fake it until you make it" for a short time.

While still grieving *and* holding a grudge, I purchased my first home on my own, bought an overpriced vehicle, started a new career, and became a "Glam-Ma".

I appeared successful outwardly, but inwardly I was still stuck in "yesterday" and heavy grief because I had not yet forgiven. My mind was still on all that everyone did or didn't do. What they said and what they didn't and should have said.

I still wanted *them* to "pay" for their unfair treatment of me. I had cut off all communication between us and others. That was the one thing I was relieved to experience in death: I did not have to remain connected to anyone who had caused harm to me emotionally and psychologically.

"Good riddance" was the verbiage in my gratitude journal and mind.

Now, I will admit I wasn't always easy to get along with either. I came into my marriage with plenty of insecurities about being a new wife. And others knew it. They knew what buttons to push to get me. Thankfully, as I strengthened my relationship with Christ and myself, they found out my "buttons" could no longer be easily manipulated.

* * *

One morning, as I was driving to my new job, I heard Holy Spirit whisper, "You can't move forward looking back."

Immediately, I was convicted. While I appeared to be "moving forward," the unforgiveness kept me from moving into my full healing potential.

While I had been upset those many months, I was constantly being reminded to pray for my enemies and to bless those that cursed me. I had not been doing that consistently. But, I started. Taking that step is what made me receptive to the conviction that I couldn't move forward while yet holding onto bitterness and unforgiveness.

***

So, later that day, I mustered up the humility and strength to reach out to one of the in-laws. The moment she answered the phone, I tensed up. As I heard the very sound of her voice, I could feel myself choking up.

The family member's voice activated many memories: Me & Steve's trips to Arkansas, the dirt roads and railroad track across the street from his mom's home, the "Mom and Pop" just up the road where we'd walk to get "rag bologna"; the small, country church that had the private cemetery where Steve and his sister were buried.

When I heard her voice, all these thoughts flooded my mind.

I could sense the feel of her embrace, the smell of her house, and the food she cooked. It also brought back the reality that Steve was no longer alive, as every trip we made to that area was to see them.

I was not prepared to feel the overwhelming urge to cry as I did while we talked on the phone. As she waited for me to speak, I let everything out that I had been harboring. I let her know how unfair and unjust she had been in not properly communicating to me. I mentioned the rumors.

SUDDENLY *Single* WIDOW'S EDITION

On and on I went.

She was silent. But, then she began to speak.

She shared the grievances that she had with me. She could not admit at that time that she was wrong. She apologized half-heartedly and said she didn't want me grieving for a long time over Steve. She encouraged me to move forward with my life.

This frustrated me, as I felt as if she was minimizing my love for him. But at that moment, I learned to accept what she could give at the time.

Sometimes, we want to force others to accept responsibility for their wrong when they have not yet reconciled it within themselves. She felt justified to do what she did then; I felt justified in my actions.

I managed to hold back the tears while speaking with her, but after we hung up, I began to sob heavily. Steve's memories and sounds were embodied in her voice, and it was a bit much for me.

I couldn't shake it.

It could have been a better call . Yet, I was proud of myself for taking a step toward forgiveness. I was still waiting to be reconciled with her due to not receiving a sincere apology. Nonetheless, I had to make the hard but necessary decision to forgive.

Don't hold up your healing and freedom waiting for an apology that may never come. Decide to forgive. It may not be easy, but you can do it. Forgiving does not mean allowing the offender to come back into your life or space quickly. There will need to be a re-establishment of boundaries. Without healthy boundaries, the relationship cannot heal. If a person cannot accept personal responsibility for their wrong actions or blames you for everything but can't see their part, they are unhealthy, and the time is not suitable to reconnect with them.

"If it is possible, as far as it depends on you, live in peace with everyone." **(Romans 12:18, New International Version)**. Sometimes, in order for there to be peace in a situation, there must be a separation.

However, the phone call was a start.

* * *

Each week from that point, we'd call each other so that she could speak with the girls. Later, I began to mail pictures of the children and the drawings the baby would make at the daycare. My family told me that she saved these pictures and posted them on her refrigerator.

After a few months of these steps toward forgiveness, the family member stopped calling. I reached out to check on her and to find out why we had not heard from her in several weeks. When she answered, she'd been ill. She'd had surgery and was recovering.

I let her know that I would be praying for her.

Praying this time wasn't a strain as I had forgiven her. God had done a great job in my heart. I felt nothing but genuine tenderness and kindness toward her.

I had forgiven...for real.

So, to hear her news saddened me. I knew God had healed my hurt and the bitter memories as I felt genuine concern, not satisfaction. Had I heard this news before I had forgiven, I don't know what my response would have been.

Yet, God knew that for me to accurately reflect Him, I had to give her what He gave me. Forgiveness.

* * *

In that same conversation, the individual finally admitted and took responsibility for her part in the breakdown of our relationship after Steve's passing. She sincerely apologized and reassured me that she loved the children and me.

I apologized again to her and let her know I appreciated her. I told her that I accepted her apology and had forgiven her. I told her I loved her as well, and we ended the conversation with her speaking with the baby.

A short time later, this person passed away. Her death caused another level of grief as it was like losing Steve again since they were family.

I was so grateful for our last conversation before she passed away. That previous conversation freed both of us from the bitter chains of unforgiveness.

The moment I chose to forgive was the moment I chose to heal.

When I consciously decided to forgive the wrongs enacted against me and lived out forgiveness, I began to see God's hand in my life. My prayer life felt more effortless and less constrained. I started to soar in my new career in healthcare, being featured and recognized in several newsletters; I began to get promotions on my job. My influence began to grow on the job.

No one at my job even knew what I was facing, as I never told them until a year and a half later. I knew there was a time and place for everything, and the workplace wasn't it—exercise common sense in how

SUDDENLY *Single* WIDOW'S EDITION

much personal information you disclose at your place of employment.

My children became happier as I was no longer short-tempered and snappy. My countenance began to relax, and I stopped looking like I was "mean mugging" everyone when I was just in chill mode. My whole life began to turn around for the better, and I was now free to move forward.

How have you found forgiveness to play a part in your healing process?

Say this with me: "*While I am still hurt, I choose to forgive. I know that forgiveness is a daily choice and does not mean that I must be reconciled to the individual, especially, if there is no change in behavior. Forgiveness is hard, but it CAN be done. I can do ALL things through Christ who gives me strength. Today, I choose to forgive and to LIVE!*"

"Healing is a choice. The thing you fear most has no power. Your fear of it is what has the power. Facing the truth really will set you free."

~Oprah Winfrey

CHAPTER VI:

Widow's Fire

Fighting that "fiery" feeling? You know-the one down below that seems to reverberate sensations unexpectedly through your entire body? The one that makes you want to take a day to go "paint the town red."

You're horny!

Your spouse is no longer available to help satisfy you. HOW FRUSTRATING is that? Well, that's what we're going to address in this chapter!

You lost your loved one. You miss the physical intimacy you once shared. You are still human! I wish I did not know what 'widow's fire' was.

Well, I didn't know what it was at first. Well, I knew what "it" was, but I didn't realize there was a specific term to describe it. So, I asked a few widows what they were referring to when I first heard the word in a widow's group. "Widow's fire" is the term used to describe a burning desire for sex following a spouse's or partner's bereavement (**www.widowsfire.com**).

* * *

You can breathe.
It's normal.

As you know, the death of a spouse brings a culmination of losses. One of those losses is that of physical and sexual intimacy. What do you do when

SUDDENLY *Single* WIDOW'S EDITION

sexual intimacy is no longer an option because your spouse is no longer alive? What do you do with the pent-up sexual frustration that begs to be unleashed?

As Steve had become an "incomplete" quadriplegic, meaning that there was a severe displacement of his spinal cord which made any future movements impossible, this meant no more sexual intimacy.

** Praise Break: Steve was able to regain movement in his arms and shoulders with plenty of time and prayer after being told by the neurologist that he would never regain strength again. But God! **

While the hospital neurology team offered classes on enjoying sexual intimacy with a disabled spouse, things were not the same. We were introduced to medical devices that could aid in providing an erection for men. However, with the level of injury sustained, sex was just no longer possible.

Add to the fact that between being Steve's healthcare advocate during his hospitalization, raising children, and doing ministry, I stayed so busy that I had no real energy left for intimacy.

But that didn't mean that I didn't desire it.

I missed my man and feeling his warm body next to me.

On those nights, thoughts of "stepping out" on Steve would try to enter my mind. The idea caused me distress as I had never thought about stepping out on Steve before, yet because I was deprived of the physical intimacy and his touch, for what I knew at that time would be for the rest of my life, I felt justified in entertaining the thought. Thankfully, that's all it amounted to: a thought.

It was a moment of truth. Did I genuinely mean my vows when I quoted, "in sickness and in health, forsaking all others, until death do us part?"

My vows meant more to me than my temporary desire at that time. As bad as I wanted "it," I wasn't going to betray Steve just because of my sexual appetite. He was the man I had committed to; it would be unjust for me to step out because he could no longer satisfy my sexual desires.

My commitment wouldn't let me do it.

* * *

A few months after Steve's passing, the adrenaline of running on autopilot began to simmer. The intensity of sexual lust and desire for Steve was incredible. Everything within me wanted Steve back and to enjoy his strong arms and large hands around me.

SUDDENLY *Single* WIDOW'S EDITION

I reminisced about our last kiss. It was as if I could smell the scent of his cologne all over me again. The aroma was in the bed, pillows, and sheets. I remembered our nights of cuddling.

Now, that was no longer.

I now had to "suffer" in silence when those overwhelming urges hit me. I didn't know what to do with these unfulfilled urges. The nights that I would get these urges, I would become upset with God.

"Now, Lord, you know me...Because this is unbearable, I may have to step out and get "some". I'll ask for grace and forgiveness in the morning."

As a believer who strives to practice abstinence, this has proven to be a challenging part of being "suddenly" single again. My faith was shaken as, on these nights, I selfishly began to complain to God that had He healed Steve like I had prayed, I wouldn't have these struggles.

Due to my frustration of being single and not being able to freely have sex when I wanted to without conviction, I found myself doing what I didn't want to. I tried to keep my time and mind occupied by filling it with healthy activities such as completing two degrees in one year and starting a new career where I was excelling. I was invited to many social networking events and all these things were exciting.

Yet, it didn't replace my yearning and desire for my husband. Nor did it replace the natural desire for sex.

I know what it's like to rush into a "rebound" relationship because of "needing" someone to fill that space that your spouse left behind. I know because I did it.

A "rebound" relationship is a brief fling or relationship with someone else shortly after ending a more significant relationship. It's a time when we may be dating instead of using the time to heal and get in the right headspace for someone new (Wilson, J.M,2021).

* * *

I entered a relationship with a gentleman whom I had developed a friendship with at work. He expressed his interest and would often come upstairs from his basement office to bring me breakfast or lunch. We had a few dates outside of work, which eventually led to a physical exchange between us.

It had been a while since I had experienced Steve, so to just *experience a man again* felt good. It wasn't just about the sex. It was psychological. It was about feeling desired and wanted again. It was about belonging to another again.

SUDDENLY *Single* WIDOW'S EDITION

This man eased the sexual tension I had been carrying for several months. He fulfilled an emotional need that I had as well. He did everything I needed him to do and more when it came to having my needs met.

What I didn't expect was the overwhelming grief and betrayal I felt after the fact.

Even though Steve had been laid to rest for several months, I felt like I was cheating on him. I knew that both naturally and spiritually, death separates us from our partners, and we are no longer married to them. I understand that the "dead knows nothing."

Yet, I felt guilty as if I was still a married woman. This indicated to me that I was not ready to move forward with another person. But I wasn't ready to let go of the sexual fulfillment I had experienced either. It was exhilarating to be naked with someone new. The sex was good, and I felt "entitled" to indulge because, after all, wasn't God the one that put me in this predicament?

When we are grieving, our faith may be shaken, but God is not to blame.

Stay with God.

God had already given me His word that He was going to "heal Steve," but not in the way that I expected.

There are levels of healing that may not always include the individual being healed on this side of heaven.

God had been gracious to us, as it was torture for Steve to be bedridden and unable to care for himself and his family. He was no longer able to do the things he once enjoyed. In some ways, death was a gift.

Praise Break: Through prayer, Steve was weaned off the trach and the feeding tube!

I am grateful for God's grace in our time of need. God is not as quick to judge nor condemns us as we often do ourselves or each other.

While God knows I have my physical limitations, He also knew I was self-medicating my grief and loneliness with this person. God and I both knew that while I enjoyed this gentleman's company, there was no future for me with him. God gently advised me that my pain didn't negate my obligation to obey His Word.

In other words, my pain was not an excuse to do whatever I chose. He understood my pain. He is my Comforter; His Word protects us naturally and spiritually. To protect my heart as well as not cause hurt to others, I had to learn new coping techniques and skills to harness my passions. I admit that I have not been perfect in this area, but I know how to repent, forgive myself, and move forward.

Coping Techniques

The coping techniques that I have found personally to be effective are dancing (which I LOVE to do; plus it's also a form of exercise), exercising, taking up a new hobby, and plenty of self-care.

When I feel alone, I either go out on a "me-date" or join a few of my close girlfriends, and we have dinner together. Getting outdoors and walking or playing with my daughters has been helpful.

But, none of these things can satisfy certain needs.

Self-care for me also looked like going back to school to complete my college education. Since Steve's passing, I acquired two associate degrees and a few certifications.

I also began educating myself through a Christian dating session on how to date effectively. The class was sooo good as it didn't just inform me how to get a date, but how to prepare and heal yourself as an individual before stepping out on a date. I desire to remarry again as I enjoyed marriage.

The classes also reminded me what real love looked like. It's been five years since I've had to think about dating again and the world has changed so much. I have begun dating again and have dated several great men, but nothing serious evolved out of these interactions other than friendship and a few rendezvous.

Learning To Date Again

When I began dating again, I learned that the standards we have of widows dating and remarrying, especially in the household of faith, are different for the widowers.

It seems to be acceptable for men to remarry within a short period without question. But when a woman begins to date moving towards remarriage, it's frowned upon. The woman is often advised to "busy" herself in ministry, yet the Word permits the younger widows to remarry and bear children so that they won't become busybodies.

While this principle is not "mandatory," it is a practical one as there are certain desires that younger widows and widowers are more prone to than someone who may have a little more years under their belt.

I've known several instances where when a male in leadership or otherwise lost their spouse to death, they were remarried within a month or two. Yet, six years later, here I am still widowed and dating.

SUDDENLY *Single* WIDOW'S EDITION

I must be transparent and state that while I do desire to remarry again, I have learned how to enjoy singleness again. I had been single longer than I was married, so while adjusting to single life has its challenges, it's been a little easier to adapt to.

I had been a single mother for fourteen years before marriage, so I learned how to be self-sufficient and independent. This has made it a little easier for me to relax in dating and take my time to get to know people.

I understand that readapting to singleness may be a little more difficult for those who were married longer than I was. I've known other widows and widowers who've known marriage for most of their life, so adjusting to being single has posed a real challenge for them.

I have compassion for them as I pray, as they have for me. The impact of the loss of the partnership, the additional finances, and the manual labor, can be very taxing, whether you've been married a year and a half or fifty years!

Finding Self-Love Again

Another means of learning to appreciate and honor my natural desires was to learn more about myself. I discovered a new relationship with myself and my body by taking the time to get to know it. I've learned the power and strength that I carry as a woman physically and spiritually.

Women are life-givers in so many ways and that includes our sexuality. We bring life to our future spouses through our bodies and the intimacy that we provide them when the time for love is ripe.

Comprehending the power of our femininity and masculinity and how it fits into God's context of love causes us to want to wait until we remarry before sharing our bodies mindlessly.

No judgment or condemnation-we're human and we give in sometimes. The desire for sex and intimacy is a God-given and ordained gift that is reserved for the marriage bed as that is where it holds the most power.

As a widowed individual who has struggled with the "widow's fire," I have found it to be extremely frustrating when I hear married couples state, "Just wait on God," or make suggestions that I was "thirsty" due to a natural desire that needed to be quenched.

Ok, so maybe that does sound a little "thirsty" because thirst is usually ignited when there is dehydration somewhere.

Ok?!

No one knows what it feels like to be able to enjoy the beauty of physical intimacy with your spouse for

SUDDENLY *Single* WIDOW'S EDITION

however long you had them and be expected to *suddenly* go "cold turkey".

No one, except another widow/er, can understand what it's like to try to hang on with everything you've got to not fall into sexual temptation and lust because you DO love God and want to honor Him with your body.

Just because you or I desire a spouse, whether for intimacy or not, does not mean that we are "thirsty" or are not "waiting on God." Just because you choose to "upgrade" yourself and go on a date, doesn't mean that you are not "waiting on God."

God's definition of "wait" is different from ours. "Wait" in Hebrew is *gavah* (H6960), which means, "*to bind together.*"

It is a proactive word. It does not mean sitting idly in a corner being quiet and waiting patiently. It's about binding together with Him in agreement with His best for your life. This may look like changing something about yourself (hairstyle, wardrobe, furthering your education, going out on a date, etc.) to prepare for the next season of your life.

Now, I may step on some toes, but preparing does not mean having sex while dating. Dating doesn't mean getting to know someone for the sole purpose of having sex. But let's be honest. It HAPPENS! Sex is very powerful and enjoyable. While we don't get to judge, we must be sensitive enough towards widows and widowers to understand that there's a big transition after the death of a spouse.

> **What you were used to, you no longer have and that is a STRUGGLE! You had no idea that your marriage was going to end like that. You didn't know that it was going to be early when your spouse would pass away.**

You didn't get married and expect that after a few years, your spouse would die. You were expecting to get old and gray with them.

It is very, very hard, especially for newly widowed/single Christian people, because it takes everything we've got to hang in there and not give in to the sexual temptations. Instead, we are often met with judgment and condemnation from the married because we are now single. Those with spouses seem to feel like we're now after theirs!

We don't want 'em!

SUDDENLY *Single* WIDOW'S EDITION

Encourage The Widows/ers

We need to get behind each other and encourage the other that they can make it! We still need to treat each other like the kings and queens we are whether we have given in to temptation or not.

Start lifting the arms of the widowed and support them by fasting and praying with them instead of condemning them! And don't just pray that God keeps us single so we can add benefit to your ministry while you are with your husband or wife! Pray that God will send us our next spouse! We are vulnerable in our time of widowhood.

Many who are married cannot imagine what it's like to lose a spouse and the turmoil that comes along with it. We must be mindful to be compassionate towards one another.

When our loved one passed, it changed our entire lifestyle. The Word teaches that the younger widows are to be married again as it prevents them from

---

We lack compassion and mercy. We frown upon everything that doesn't look like what we think it should be. We must be careful that we show compassion towards each other.

becoming idle busybodies, doing things that they ought not to do.

Yet, in our vulnerability, we strive to keep our sexual integrity as best we can. Especially, if you are wanting to be remarried. I want to be remarried. Knowing this has motivated me to establish boundaries that will keep me sexually pure until I meet my next spouse.

Spend time with God. Get to know Him intimately and allow Him to purify you so that you will be prepared for your next. We can sometimes delay the blessing that God wants to bring into our lives by entangling ourselves with those who don't want anything but sexual intimacy from us...

YES, EVEN IN THE CHURCH!

"There's someone who's been waiting and praying to God for a good woman or a good man. It doesn't matter how many are compromising and giving themselves away sexually because they carry "swagger" or charisma. YOU stand strong. At the end of the day, those who persist in doing whomever and whatever they like will end up by themselves!" -Coach Louis

Not to mention, there are still physical consequences of sleeping around..no matter your age. Don't forget that **STDS** are still on the rise and many common ones are now resistant to the original antibiotics. You don't want to enter a new marriage having to explain the physical repercussions of poor sexual decisions.

SUDDENLY *Single* WIDOW'S EDITION

However, if you've contracted an incurable STI, there are a few ways to share this delicate information in a responsible, mature, and honest way with the new person. You'll want to ensure that you are upfront, transparent, and have resources available to share with your new person. You will also want to ensure the timing and location is right for sharing.

Some suggested verbiage from Healthline is:

Before we hook up, we should talk status. I'll go first. My last STI screen was (INSERT DATE), and I'm (POSITIVE/NEGATIVE) for (INSERT STI(s)). How about you?"

"I have (INSERT STI). I'm taking medication to manage/treat it. I thought it's something you need to know before we take things further. I'm sure you have questions, so fire away." (2022).

It's a tough conversation, but a necessary one, as you want to start your new relationship built on trust. You also want to be safe. Especially at a time when you're sexually and emotionally vulnerable.

My friend, these are some healthy coping mechanisms that I've found that help me to stay focused and keep my sexual, physical, emotional, and spiritual integrity intact. And to help keep the fire down.

What have you found to help manage your *fiery* nights?

CHAPTER VII:

Another Chance

At A Happy Ending

Speaking of desire, there may come a time when you may desire to date, court, and/or remarry again. It is your decision when and if you choose to date or remarry.

You deserve to experience happiness again whether it's with or without a partner. I have heard those who've lost spouses say they never want to marry or fall in love again. That is your choice. I support you and agree with it if that is your desire.

I also support and agree with those who choose to take another chance at love. I believe no one was created to do life alone.

"For two are better than one because they have a good return for their labor." **(Ecclesiastes 4:9-12**, NIV)

Again, dating doesn't mean getting to know someone just to have sex. The "hookup" culture is real. Accurate dating is to find out who this man or woman is. Do they want to be a husband or a wife?

For the Christians (believers): Are they born again?

When dating with the intention of marriage, you're not looking to be a "Boo" or a booty call.

"If you're looking to remarry and he is not husband material, you're not looking for him.

SUDDENLY *Single* WIDOW'S EDITION

If she is not wife material, you are not looking for her. You need to make a "do" and "don't" list: if they don't fit the qualifications, they're not on your list. Don't allow your heart to get involved with the "look" or the "charisma." If they're not looking for a wife or husband, and you are, they are not the one."-Coach Geri Louis

Marriage provides protection and security like no other human relationship. However, I do believe that you also need healthy friendships with people of the same sex. Oftentimes, when we begin to date again, we tend to shut others out.

Our friendships can help us to maintain balance and accountability. I have close friends who will provide honest feedback about individuals I may be dating. The accountability helps me remember the important questions I should ask while dating:

"What is your relationship like with your parents? Your kids?"

"Do you wish to have any more children?"

"How do you manage your finances?"

"Do you have any STDS?"

"Do you believe in God?"

If they've been divorced: "*What did you learn from the breakup?*" *How did you grow from your mistakes?*"

So on and so forth.

* * *

If one of the spouses' stumbles, they have the other to help uplift and support them. While the marriage is not independent of external help, there's a unique and sacred bond that is built between the two lovers.

A spouse is made to be a "helpmeet" for each other. "Help meet" the need. "Help meet" the goals.

Moving Forward

Often, especially widows, find that they receive harsh judgment when they decide to move forward with dating. It's hard to move on and no one should judge you if you decide to move forward in happiness after such grim circumstances.

We often find that judgment may come from our in-laws, the church, well-meaning friends, etc. Widows tend to receive greater criticism about dating or remarrying than widowers. I'm not sure why this is,

SUDDENLY *Single* WIDOW'S EDITION

but there seems to be a double standard when it comes to remarriage for the widowed.

Dating in this new era can be taxing. There are so many dating apps where you can meet other singles and widows. Honestly, I have not desired to marry a widower. At least, if he is not healed as I would not want to be compared to his previous spouse. This is one area that I had to do my work in as well.

Though imperfect, as all of us beings are, Steve had a lot of great qualities, which are a bit difficult to find in this day and time. Notice that I said a "bit difficult" but not "impossible."

I had to surrender the notion that every man who I dated had to be "just like Steve."

When you go into a dating relationship holding on to what you had, you are not open to what could be. Take the opportunity to meet another great love. It is unfair to yourself and the individual whom God may have sent to help heal and love you. Who knows? You may find another who can love you greater. Nothing is impossible.

I believe that love is possible if desired. You must ensure you are healed enough to know and accept that for yourself.

In other instances, there may be hesitancy in courting and remarriage. We may be afraid to be with someone new as we feel that it may take away the love we had for our late spouses.

Or there's a real fear that we might find ourselves falling in love even greater with the new person. We feel like no one can compare to our late loved ones. I struggled with not comparing any new men I dated with Steve. While I knew that Steve was not perfect, he possessed a lot of great qualities that are not easily found in the "modern" men of today.

As mentioned in previous chapters, Steve knew how to hunt, fish, cook, and clean and he was kind! Steve was not a pushover, but he never raised his voice at me or our daughters.

Another Try At Dating

Recently, I stepped out of my comfort zone and dated a younger guy. This was different for me because since I graduated from high school, I've only dated older men. Most men that I dated were ten to twenty years older than me. Now, here I was dating this man who was sixteen years younger than me.

We met at church and quite honestly, I didn't pay much attention to him. For one, I don't go to church to search for men (Note: I didn't say that I was *blind*...haha). For two, when he approached me, I

SUDDENLY *Single* WIDOW'S EDITION

thought he was much younger than he was because he had a very youthful face.

From the beginning, this man seemed to be very attentive. He was friendly, quite sexy and had a strong, hard body. He was a cutie and was very talented. He seemed to be very responsible and family oriented.

He also stated that he was desirous and preparing himself to be married. I was who and what he wanted.

Yet, after about a month of dating, I noticed that he carried an imbalance of excess responsibilities that caused him great stress. With this stress, came rage and "lash outs."

He became emotionally and verbally abusive toward me. When I would let him know how he made me feel and established boundaries, this upset him further. Yet, thankfully, because he had a relationship with God, he became convicted and came back to apologize for his behavior. He has also began seeking therapy to help him better organize priorities and reduce his stress.

However, I removed myself from the situation and the individual. When you're dating, if helping someone begins to negatively impact you, please step back and encourage the individual to seek help

After this experience, I became "hungry" for Steve. Steve had never been rough with me a day in his life. Steve had my back, and I had his. I could talk to him, and he would correct me when needed.

I began to lament and despise the fact that I was even in the position to date again. I took a moment to rest from dating as this guy had been number seven since Steve passed six years ago. I needed time to re-establish my standards and to exhale after dating this guy.

He just wasn't the one.

Still Desiring Marriage

Despite this experience, I still desire to court and remarry again. I refuse to let one bad experience stop me from desiring and having real love again. I will never allow anyone to have that type of control over my love life.

I have no regrets about love, only experience. I learned how to make better choices in love. I know that just like you, I am deserving of genuine and good love from a good person.

You do not have to settle.

The goal is to be established with someone who loves and appreciates you. If they do not love God, they will not know how to love you properly. They may not be as strong in faith as you, but that doesn't mean they don't love God. Pray and ask God.

If you desire to date or remarry again, do it. Do it with the right person at the right time for *you*. Make sure that you are upfront with the new individual that you begin to date. Be honest about your intentions.

Being in love with someone unprepared to commit can be painful for all involved. For those who are healing from the death of their spouse but yearning for the companionship of the opposite sex and are just looking for sex, be honest.

Your transparency upfront will help prevent you or the person you're dating from becoming "collateral damage".

When I dated the first gentleman after Steve, I was craving companionship. I knew that I eventually wanted to remarry, but I wasn't sure that I wanted it to be this guy or even right now. I was still battling twinges of guilt after moving forward.

Avoid The Rebound

In other words, I was still healing, and I knew I wasn't ready. Yet, this guy became a 'rebound' relationship for me because I craved physical touch and intimacy. Most of us know what a rebound relationship is as either we've been the 'rebound' or we've made some one else the 'rebound.'

As we're healing and rediscovering ourselves, we don't want to leave a trail of damage behind us. It's wise to be self-aware and permit yourself to heal before moving forward with dating.

* * *

In the case of the gentleman, I dated immediately after Steve's departure, he left with a broken heart. I hadn't meant to mislead this man. I had been upfront with him and let him know that I knew our relationship was a rebound for me. He acknowledged that he also did not have any plans to remarry again, which he knew was my eventual desire.

He had gone through a difficult divorce and became anti-marriage. The institution of marriage in and of itself is not the *issue*.

There are legitimate and legal reasons for divorce, such as adultery and abuse. However, we must be careful not to "throw the baby out with the bathwater." I am referring to throwing out "marriage," due to the hurt we've experienced with one individual-especially if we desire to experience another chance at love.

SUDDENLY *Single* WIDOW'S EDITION

Nonetheless, I've enjoyed dating and getting the opportunity to meet and make new friends. I have met many nice gentlemen who I have enjoyed dinner and laughter with. Some of these men, I continue in friendship with. Yet, the dating/courting scene is a little different than when I dated before meeting Steve.

With the COVID pandemic and the global lockdown, the use of social media has almost tripled. In this new era, many are meeting their new loves through mediums such as Facebook, Instagram, and other dating apps and sites.

I know of a very successful couple who met through Facebook, and they have since married and are doing life, business, and ministry well. They are excelling in life!

I have met many great men through "friending" on social media, both locally as well as out of the state and country. Now, of course, dating across the country can be a little more complicated. But it can be successful and lead to marriage when God is in it.

As I continue to learn about myself and move forward into dating with the intent to remarry, I find that I must *reawaken* the "wife" in me. I have found that I have gotten settled into singleness and now must shift my mindset from being 'single' to being a "wife in waiting."

Jan Mitchell

Anticipating A New Beginning

By faith, I believe and stand on the thought that 2023 is going to be the year that I wed. Currently, I don't have a steady relationship with anyone, but I believe that as I continue to keep my heart open and make room for love, it will happen.

I know many times when we've lost our spouse, we feel as if we've lost our "soulmate" or our one and only. While we will never forget our dear loved ones, I believe Steve loved me so much that he would want me to be happy and move forward with my life, including remarrying.

Steve knew me intimately. He was acquainted with my heartbeat. He knew my goals, dreams, and desires that I had individually as well as the ones we had for each other. He would want me to be happy just as I would want him had I passed on first. I would not want him to linger in grief and be unable to move forward. I would want him to be happy.

Again: Release the guilt of moving forward. Just because you choose to heal does not mean you have forgotten your spouse. It simply means you have decided to LIVE.

CHAPTER VIII:

Discovering You

In A New Season:
Healed, Whole & Moving Forward

Healed. Whole. Moving Forward.

A significant turning point in my healing journey was finally allowing myself to feel my pain. As long as I numbed my pain with busyness and life, I thought I was okay. Well, I wasn't.

Grief is painful. And I was not too fond of it.

I didn't want to be labeled as one of 'those people' who gets stuck in the cycle of grief and never seems to truly process grief properly. I didn't want to *embrace* my pain because to me that meant I was comfortable with it.

I didn't want to be known as a 'widow' all my life. I just wanted to get on with life, cry when I needed to and keep it moving!

Yet, until I slowed down and gave myself permission to grieve, I wouldn't heal. The moment I allowed myself to *feel*, I began to heal. After all, aren't those blessed with comfort who dare to mourn?

I didn't realize that I was forfeiting the grace to heal by being silent about my pain. I was silent with myself. I was silent with others. I was silent with God. I know what it feels like to be afraid to share your story with others because of any raw emotions you're scared it might trigger. After all, if you're still feeling those emotions, you may not be as far along in your healing process as you thought, right?

Not necessarily true.

I found that the moment I opened and faced my fear, the freer I became. The more I shared, the load of pain I carried began to lighten. Not because I had numbed myself to what I felt while sharing, but rather the opposite.

I received more support and grace when I displayed my humanity and frailty. Telling my story also provided me with a means of "measurement" of my healing. I didn't realize that as grief comes in waves, healing comes in layers.

For instance, after Steve passed away at the hospital, I made it a point never to step foot or drive by that facility again. I had no reason to visit, and I didn't live or work near the facility.

So, there was no need to waste gas, right?

I appreciated the staff who tended to Steve before his passing, but the fact that Steve died there caused me great anxiety.

Facing My Fears

One day, I received a phone call from a friend whose son worked in pharmaceutical sales. His son was being flown on assignment to Indianapolis to provide sales to the radiology team regarding a new product.

As the son had never been to the city before, the father asked if I wouldn't mind showing his son around.

This particular hospital consists of several smaller hospitals across Indianapolis. The address that the young man provided me was to the north location. I was relieved that this was not where Steve had taken his last breath.

I was excited about meeting this young man, and we agreed to meet for lunch at the hospital. Upon arrival, I called him, and he tried to guide me to where he was located. I couldn't find him anywhere in the lobby where we had agreed to meet. After a few minutes of speaking with him, I asked him to describe a landmark in the hospital. After a few failures, we discovered that he had given me the wrong hospital address. He was at the location where Steve had died.

Something died inside of me.

I had not stepped foot in that location in six years, and I was okay with that. Now, I was being "**asked**" to confront my anxieties.

I wasn't sure how I would feel when I arrived. Would I freak out and burst into tears in the parking lot? My heart was racing, but I began talking to God as I drove from the north to the west side of town. I shared with God my fears and distress. As I began to pray, I began to calm down. I reminded myself it was a new day and

SUDDENLY *Single* WIDOW'S EDITION

a new time. And I had been given a chance to experience a unique opportunity.

As I parked and tentatively walked into the hospital that had become our second home, I whispered an additional prayer to God, asking for strength. As I met the rather handsome young man and we began to head to the cafeteria, I felt at ease. I didn't feel the panic or heart palpitations that I expected to feel.

As we ordered our food, "Mr. Fine" and I sat at one of the tables I had often seated at during my many visits to see Steve.

I felt peace.

I felt joy as we indulged in laughter and great conversation! I learned so much about "Mr. Fine ." We had a delightful time together.

The networking and even the hospital food were good! We took a picture together, which made one passerby note, "You two look good together!"

They didn't know, nor was I going to tell, that I was close to twenty years this young man's junior. That just means that I look really good for my age, and we'll leave it at that!

Haha!

As I drove home later that afternoon, I realized that I had conquered another level of healing. Had I not faced my fear, I would not have experienced that new layer of healing. If I had not exposed myself to the fear, I would not know how much I've grown in my grief journey. It would be best if you allowed grief to complete its work in you holistically.

Understanding The Healing Wave

It wasn't enough to heal from the physical absence created by Steve's death. I also needed to heal and recover from the memories attached to the circumstances, places, and things that all reminded me of what happened.

If I could hurt, then I could heal.

I felt so accomplished after leaving that hospital. I had made a major stride in my grief journey that day. I shared my victorious report with loved ones. The overwhelming encouragement and support from my family and friends was extraordinary

---

If we keep silent, grief has free course to wreak havoc on our mental, physical, emotional, and spiritual health. But with exposure, comes release. Freedom leads to healing.

SUDDENLY *Single* WIDOW'S EDITION

Prior to this moment, there were many nights where I would silently relive the trauma from Steve's fall to his last breath. I was not healing. I was dying inwardly over and over again.

I had entrapped myself in grief by my silence.

But, just as my silence bound me, my speaking up liberated me. An anonymous writer stated, "You're so hard on yourself. Take a moment. Sit back—Marvel at your life. At the **GRIEF** that softened you, the heartache that **WISENED** you, and the suffering that **STRENGTHENED** you. Despite everything, you still **GROW**. Be proud of this" (author unknown).

It's okay to talk about your story. There are those who need to hear what you have to say.

* * *

One day, I decided to stop serving grief and instead allow grief to serve **ME**! I know that as bad as it hurt, Steve would want me to honor his life by healing, moving forward & living.

Death is a thief and a robber.

Part of the healing journey includes learning how to reclaim your life and identity after the loss of your spouse.

When we got married, like you and your loved one, Steve and I had dreams that we shared, goals, and future aspirations. A lot of our plans included "us" and "we," including our children. Death canceled or shifted half of those plans.

I had to learn how to reset.

Rediscovering My Identity

When Steve passed, I lost a part of my identity. The most significant loss was my role or position as "wife ." I am still a mother, supervisor, author, and all these other titles. But, I am no longer "Mrs. Mitchell."

Death is traumatic and leaves a gap in how we view life and the perception that we have of ourselves. Therefore, we need to take time to rediscover ourselves. According to the Merriam-Webster Online Dictionary, the word rediscover means, "to discover again; something that has been ignored or forgotten or a do-over."

In becoming "Mrs. Mitchell," I had laid aside many dreams and goals to build "ours".

Rediscovering ourselves begs us to ask the question:

"Where do I go from here?"

"What am I going to do now?"

SUDDENLY *Single* WIDOW'S EDITION

Rediscovering requires us to be honest about where we are and where we want to be

Rediscovery starts from the inside.

You can't get another mate and feel better about yourself. If there was hurt or pain from the late spouse, be honest with yourself and give yourself time to heal. Death is not easy to get over and everyone's experience will not be the same.

* * *

As I mentioned in previous chapters, there were some insecurities that I battled with at the beginning of my marriage. Part of those insecurities was that I didn't feel good enough to be married. This made me difficult to live with in the early stages of our marriage as I was hypersensitive towards outside women who paid him any attention.

We had happy moments, but I wasn't thrilled because I didn't know how to love myself. My insecurity made it difficult for me to accept his love for me. Even when he would express that he loved me, my mind and heart couldn't fully absorb it. I didn't believe it because it didn't "feel" like love. I held an immature view of love and I didn't know who I was.

This put a strain on our relationship at times.

Knowing and loving yourself is imperative before entering or re-entering a marriage.

Yet, in every interaction I had with Steve, he taught me that love is not a feeling, but an action. Love is as love does, *not* says. Even though I was a full grown adult in my early thirties, when Steve and I married, I had not allowed God to heal and grow my perspective of what **real** love was.

God used Steve to "heal" me. By the time Steve departed, I had grown to understand what real love looked like.

Sometimes, God will pair us with someone who can "heal" us.

Healing While Grieving

But now, I was shifting into another chapter of my identity, and this required me to be honest with myself.

I had to be honest that I was hurting and depressed. I had to be honest that my faith was out of whack because God didn't heal Steve as I had prayed. I had to be honest about if I wanted to continue in ministry or not.

I had to be honest that I wasn't sure if I wanted to be remarried or just wanted to enjoy sex when I needed

SUDDENLY *Single* WIDOW'S EDITION

it and call it a day. When you're healing and learning to shift into a new identity following something as traumatic as death, you must allow yourself time to process the change.

* * *

Recouping from the loss of my identity as a wife and discovering what my talents were wasn't easy. Six years after his death, I am still learning and rediscovering myself daily, but I enjoy what I find out about myself.

I learned that I like to write. I learned that I have more courage and strength than I initially thought I had. I learned that I am resilient.

I realized that I could *create new boundaries for who I was becoming.* And I could remove the old expectations of who I *was*. As I rediscovered myself, I found new courage to say "No" to the things, places, and people that did not fit where I was headed. I had to press the "stop" button even on myself and what others wanted me to do so that I could take time to rediscover **Jan**. I like this new me!

* * *

Death and healing gave me a new perspective on life. In rediscovering myself, I learned I needed to finish what I had started. Life is so short, and God has invested too much inside of me for it to go to waste. For me, this meant furthering my education. I made valedictorian at one of the schools which I attended.

I started college in my early 20s but still needed to finish. I never imagined that I would be returning to school 20 years later. I always kept a decent-paying job, but now I desired more. Now, here I am with two degrees accomplished in the same year!

I also took time to learn what loving me looked like. This meant sitting down and writing out what I liked and didn't like. As we evolve, our desires change. What I discovered about the "new" me no longer matched who I was before. Death had changed me. It grew me up. It showed me that life and marriage was a gift and a privilege.

Part of my healing journey was recognizing that while I loved my husband dearly, he was not the "end all" of my life. He played a vital and essential part in my life and heart, but he could not replace God.

I recall the night I finally came to terms with the fact that Steve was going to pass. As I was wailing and mourning the impending death, I remember Holy Spirit reminding me that "before Steve was, I Am ."

What that meant was that God was the only constant in my life. From the day I was born to the day I close

my eyes on this side of the earth.

SUDDENLY *Single* WIDOW'S EDITION

He was the One who watched me and walked alongside me as a child, teaching my parents how to raise and care for me. He was the One who was consistently there when I walked through so many rough patches in my life. He helped me when I was a struggling single parent.

He was the One who snatched me out of so many traps that I had put myself in and gave me a second chance at life. He was the One who reminded me of how much I was loved when I felt unlovable. He was the One who caused me to have the opportunity to become a wife. He sent me "my person", my Steve, in the right season and at the right time.

So, if God could sustain and keep me through my life's journey from birth to this period, He is more than capable of helping me and you as we move forward in life.

He reminded me, *"Jan, I never promised you that 'man' would not leave you, but I, Myself, have said that I will never leave you nor forsake you."*

God will never leave us, even when it feels like He is nowhere to be found. He's still there and listening, quietly waiting for us to ask for His healing. He's such a gentleman. He'll never force Himself on you or force you to believe Him. But, if you talk to Him, He will answer.

Jan Mitchell

The Importance Of Faith

My faith in God has been essential to my healing and moving forward. My faith did not numb me to the realities of death and grief; instead, it put it in its proper perspective. I recognize that death is a temporary part of life. I will see Steve again when it's time. But, in the meantime, I choose TO LIVE!

My faith inspired me to co-create a Christian internet talk show called "Well, Hades!!" which ministers holistically to the widowed and the single. It is now viewed worldwide on YouTube, RokuTV, and other media platforms.

My faith also caused me to birth two new businesses: *The InnovativePr Company*, which provides comprehensive customer/employee relations training to businesses and other organizations. I have over 25 years of experience in customer service. The second business is my nonprofit, "*She Moves Forward, Inc.*", which will be dedicated to assisting widows with talk &
art therapy to assist in healing and move them forward into reclaiming their joy and lives again. It will commence in the spring of 2023.

Tragedy birthed purpose into my life.

SUDDENLY *Single* WIDOW'S EDITION

* * *

Before becoming a widow, I didn't know what I wanted to do or where I was headed. I knew that I was a wife and a Mom. I was in ministry. I worked a good job, and that was it. I opted for the day-to-day grind instead of digging into purpose.

Death shifted that for me.

Steve's passing catapulted me right into the face of destiny. The experiences I gained from the many nights spent at the hospital with Steve birthed compassion in my heart for those traveling down a similar path.

Becoming a widow was not the "ministry" that I desired. I would have never chosen it. I'd rather have my husband and have a "normal" life.

But normal was not what God wanted for me. Nor do I believe it's what He wants for you. Nor would your late loved one desire it for you. They would not want you to stop living because they have moved on.

*"For I know the plans I have for **you**," declares the Lord, "plans to **prosper** you and **not to harm** you, plans to give you hope and a future." (Jeremiah 29:11, NIV)*

They would want to see you use your pain and allow it to propel you into purpose. Because they love you. I know that it may sound "cliché," but your life matters. Your purpose matters.

YOU matter.

God's Plan

I speak to the one battling depression and suicidal thoughts due to the loss of their spouse. God has a plan for your life. Your life is not over because of the heartbreak that you're experiencing right now. I know the pain seems overwhelming and the support underwhelming, but there is someone who cares about you.

Please don't give up on your life. Trouble and pain do not last always. If you are feeling suicidal, please talk to someone. Call the National Suicide Prevention Lifeline at 988.

Your presence is needed on this side of Heaven.

You are valuable, whether you remarry or choose not to. Losing a spouse does not diminish the value of who you are. You are unique and amazingly loved.

SUDDENLY *Single* **WIDOW'S EDITION**

My New Beginning

After Steve passed, I found myself changing careers. I went from working a job as a travel agent with a prestigious company to a career in healthcare. Everything I had suffered prepared me to go back and provide a new perspective on what needs to be changed in healthcare. I wanted to know how I could help contribute to both the patients' and the clinicians' needs.

I began my new career three months after Steve's passing as I became determined that I needed a switch in my life. The old job, home, and cars all reminded me of what I had with Steve. My life had now changed, and I needed a change of pace. I needed a fresh start.

So, I started my journey in healthcare as a patient access professional. The patient access professional role has many facets. It could be the person you speak to at the registration desk, who checks you in in the emergency room, or who answers the phones to get you scheduled with your provider.

Speaking of which, as a widow or widower, please don't forget to take care of your physical health.

Continue or start seeing a primary care physician or OB-GYN (for the ladies). For the men, don't forget your annual physicals and prostate check. See your dentist twice a year and restart your eye examinations.

When looking to heal and move forward, we cannot just do it in one facet of our lives, as grief impacts every part of our lives.

Cardiomyopathy, aka "broken heart syndrome," is real. You want to stay on top of your health so that you don't short-circuit your life prematurely.

As a patient access professional, I scheduled patient appointments. It wasn't a hard job, but it required patience and compassion. It also put me in the place I needed to be. Most times, when patients called in, they were overwhelmed or sick, and they often took this out on us, who answered the phones.

We need grace too.

Yet, we smile through our troubles so that we can be of service to the patient. Please be mindful of this the next time you call your doctor's office. You may just be talking to another widow(er). Remember grace.

Though imperfect, I strive to be respectful to those on the other side of the phone with any establishment. I have over 25 years of customer service under my belt, so I strive to be diligent in "doing unto others as I would have them do unto me."

SUDDENLY *Single* **WIDOW'S EDITION**

My Time For Promotion

After a year and a half, I was promoted to senior patient access associate. This meant I had more responsibilities, such as mentoring the new hires and assisting my supervisor with other duties.

I loved the opportunity to serve in a greater capacity as I knew that I was on assignment to do what God was calling me to do. Knowing my purpose kept me motivated. There were days I would drive to work, and the thought of how I ended up in healthcare would cause tears to stream down my face. I would cry and pray as I headed to work. When I would pull into the employee parking garage, I would wipe my face, fix my makeup, and head inside with a smile.

No one knew until a year later that I had become a widow. But, in healthcare, we're often asked what's our story or our "why," which provokes us to share why we chose a career in healthcare. This is a strategic method that helps keep us connected to purpose on stressful days. This is how my boss learned my story.

Being promoted also provided me exposure to the C-suite executives who quickly learned my name and the level of excellence that I strive for daily. Every day, I would pray and ask God to help me to be a person of good character and integrity. Some days were easier than others to live out.

But, on my tough days, this prayer was a shield for me and it paid off. I didn't have to " kiss butt" or force my way into the presence of great leaders. My passion, integrity, gift of customer service, and the purposes of God opened the doors for me. I just did my part, which was to show up with integrity and to do my best.

At the beginning of my new career, I struggled with my attendance as I was still grieving Steve, and at the same time, my baby girl was diagnosed with epileptic seizures, just like Steve had. In those days, I was not yet eligible to qualify for FMLA. Staying home to take care of her when she had an episode meant my attendance was impacted. However, getting additional support from my family to assist on baby girl's sick days helped me to get out of the attendance rut. After all, I knew that I was "in purpose", and I could not afford to lose what God had established me in.

Yet, I knew my baby's health was the top priority. Thankfully, through prayer and visiting a pediatric neurologist, three years later baby girl was declared "seizure-free." She has not had an episode since.

The God who answers prayers is still alive and well!

Continuing To Soar

Another year after my first promotion, another came, and I was promoted to a patient access guide. Another year later, during the COVID-19 pandemic, God

SUDDENLY *Single* WIDOW'S EDITION

blessed me with another climb to a leadership position. The progression just kept coming! Promotion doesn't come from the east or the west. Promotion comes from God!

When I was promoted, I knew that while I was qualified, it was God's favor that opened the doors.

The best part of the last promotion was that I had been diagnosed with COVID-19 at the time of the upgrade. While I had no underlying health conditions, the virus attacked my body for four months straight. I had never been so sick in my life! I was and remained a person who would only get minor head colds. I've only had the flu once, over 20 years ago. I don't get sick quickly or often.

However, COVID took me down for four months. I didn't think that I would recover. Satan would suggest to my mind that I would die of COVID and that my children would now be without any parents.

Satan is still a liar!

Because I knew that God had destiny on His mind for me and there had been too much prophecy over my life, I knew I wasn't going to die. I let hell know that I was not going to die right now and certainly not like this!

During my illness, I only missed two days off work. We started working remotely at that time, so I didn't expose anyone to the virus. I wore a mask 24-7 in my home during the four months of being ill, so I would not affect my children. I even wore the mask at night while I slept. Yet, none of this stopped me from being promoted.

Have you noticed the pattern? Promotion comes after difficult seasons. What God has for you is FOR YOU!

Shortly after being promoted at the hospital, I was encouraged to run for Midwest Regional Delegate for the National Association of Healthcare Access Management (NAHAM).

NAHAM is an association dedicated to further educating patient access professionals across the nation. I was reluctant to apply because I didn't feel I had enough experience or qualifications to meet the need, yet I saw this as another door to purpose

So, I ran for the seat and WON!

I beat out two executives from neighboring states! I couldn't believe it! But, again when God births purpose in your life, you can't get away from it. Just embrace it.

Don't forfeit it!!

SUDDENLY *Single* WIDOW'S EDITION

* * *

Shortly after the promotion, God began to send "divine connections" into my life- good people who would help me to further discover and fulfill my purpose.

It's your turn.

My Writing Career

At the start of 2022, I met a wonderful group of ladies via Facebook™ who started and championed the first "SUDDENLY Single" anthology, by way of the visionary, Coach Venus Chandler of Kintsugi Transformations, and published by Mrs. Audrea V. Abraham of IBG (Inspired by God) Publications, Inc.

Through these ladies, I have had the chance to share my story in the first anthology, "SUDDENLY Single: Surviving the Demise of Your Relationship," and now to write this book dedicated to widows and widowers everywhere.

The Art Of Grieving

Learn the art of grieving your grief.

It starts with learning the art of grieving your grief. I know that may sound strange, so let me explain. The loss of someone or something initiates grief, right? Grief comes to help us process and sheds what once was.

When you begin to "grieve grief," you're turning it on its head. You're starting to recognize that grief has had time to run its course. You're now ready to let the grief go.

Please make no mistake about it. Letting go of grief is no easy task. After all, grief is a reminder of something we've held tightly to keep our connection to the memories of our spouses alive.

I know this may sound absurd to some and, at best, scary to others, but grieving your grief is necessary to regain your wholeness and sense of well-being. Grieving your grief means you are willing to shed what has become an old and familiar friend who has overstayed his welcome.

Have you ever invited (or not) someone to your home for dinner, when suddenly you notice that as time passes, they're getting more and more comfortable?

They may begin to take off their shoes and snuggle up on your couch, suggesting watching a super long Hallmark movie, which you don't want to watch. You've played host or hostess, and now you're tired. You want to wash the dishes and climb into bed. Yet,

SUDDENLY *Single* WIDOW'S EDITION

they are still as giddy as a lark and unable to read your body cues that it's time for them to leave.

That's grief. And it's time for him to go.

Just as one season changes to the next, a new season is in bloom waiting for you to discover it. It's a new season where the pain is not the daily norm and where you have embraced acceptance.

Because of what you experienced, you've found that you have grown and been transformed. You now have more compassion for those who have gone through loss. You no longer find fault with those who may not have known the right words to say when you were at your worst. You find that you could, and you did forgive. You've realized that you are more resilient than you knew and that you are not at fault for what happened. You find out that you are stronger than you thought.

It's time to embrace the new and more refined you. To fully embrace the new you, certified hospice and palliative care nurse Angela Morrow, RN, suggests these five steps:

1. ***Take Responsibility for Your Own Life:*** *It's time to give up any excuses for not moving forward in life and take 100% responsibility for yourself.*

2. ***Change Your Way of Thinking***: *Change negative self-talk to words of affirmation. Change your, "I can't" to "I can."*
3. ***Do Something New:*** *You wouldn't be a new you if you didn't try something new. Learn a new skill, travel to a new place, and try (healthy and safe) things you never thought you would.*
4. ***Set New Personal Goals***: *Set new goals you can begin to work towards-this will help you to stay focused on your new journey*
5. ***Help Someone Else:*** *Help someone through their journey with the lessons you learned in your time of grief. (www.verywellhealth.com) Your story is what someone else needs to hear. You may not feel as if your story is worth sharing, but I guarantee you, it is. You are the solution to someone else's problem.*

Explore Yourself

While venturing out into the new you, be patient with yourself. There will be bumps along the way as such is life.

But keep going if you experience a setback. Setbacks are only temporary setups for you to make a grand comeback! Allow yourself grace. Life is a marathon, not a 50-yard dash.

SUDDENLY *Single* WIDOW'S EDITION

While I did not know about these five principles of letting go of grief before researching content for this book, I have found that I have done each of them. Each step has been essential in aiding in my healing journey.

I took responsibility for my healing.

I finally snapped out of the stupor of grief and realized that for me to be healed, I had to participate. I couldn't continue to shuffle in my pain, making excuses for not securing my healing. It took God and a team of individuals to help hold me accountable for getting back on track and staying focused. Utilize your core people during your recovery. They will help you to stay focused on this journey of "new."

I also changed my way of thinking. This was a little harder as grief had become the new "narrative" that I married myself to. Anytime, I was late paying a bill or needed assistance in any manner, my story of how I was a widow mom of three daughters was my default conversation.

But when I started to feel disempowered by sharing my story to make excuses for not renewing my perspective, I made a change.

Again, be patient with yourself, as the change will be gradual. You will need to renew your mind daily through the Bible and other literature to learn a new way of thinking and doing.

Remember: Healing from grief is a holistic experience. It's both natural and spiritual.

Trying New Things

I tried something new.

Going back to school was trying something new because it challenged me to finally finish what I had started so many years prior.

It was a bit intimidating to return to school as forty-two-year-old woman. I was raising daughters, working, and participating in ministry.

But I got the job done. And to celebrate my accomplishments, I did something else new. I took a flight to Hawaii all by myself!

A New First For My Life

I had driven solo interstate many times before but flying solo transpacific was new for me.

But....I had the time of my life!

I met new people and indulged myself in the Hawaiian culture, which is one of love- Aloha Aina.

SUDDENLY *Single* WIDOW'S EDITION

I woke up every morning between five and six to walk the rocky shores of the Pacific Ocean and watch the sunrise.

Just me and God.

We had plenty of good conversations. I would shed a few tears as I breathed in the fresh, warm air, remembering that Steve wasn't there to enjoy it with me.

I was alone, but I was okay. And that felt good.

As it was my birthday weekend, I took myself to every highly rated restaurant on the island.

On my birthday night, I partied by myself in my condo. I blasted Shop Boyz's "Party Like A Rockstar," "Birthday" by Twista, and a few other 90's jams that I remember from my high school days.

And for those who might judge, yes, I still love and serve God! I danced my tail off as if there were fifty other people in the condo with me. I laughed and "dropped it like it was hot!" I felt FREE!

Ha-ha!

I told you earlier that dancing was something I enjoy doing. But the whole point was that I tried something new! And I was enjoying it!

JAN MITCHELL

I was learning to live again.

My new personal goals were to finish my schooling and write my first book which I did! I also traveled for the first time to San Diego and Los Angeles, California to promote the "SUDDENLY Single" movement and the efforts of NAHAM.

I spoke at my first national conference as Midwest Regional Delegate for patient access professionals. I was nervous. But, I did it, accomplishing my goal of public speaking on a national level.

I've started helping others by making the bold moves to change my career and by sharing my story. Like many of you, I was initially nervous about sharing my story because I knew that I would have to remember some tough things I had grieved over. I knew that I had healed, but I didn't want to stumble across an area that still needed healing.

The truth is, there may still be some things that make me cry when I think of this journey that I've had to endure. It started devastatingly and led to many hard nights, tears, and frustration.

But, it's a new season. And I am healed, whole and ready to experience all God & life has to offer me.

As I finish typing, with the song, "Anniversary" by Tony Toni Tone playing quietly in the background, I take a moment and reflect on all that I've experienced

SUDDENLY *Single* WIDOW'S EDITION

in this journey of losing my beloved, Stephen Lee Mitchell.

All the heartbreak that I've experienced. All the joy and laughter that we once shared. How faithful God has been to fulfill His Word that, *"All things work together for the good of them who love God and are called according to His purpose."* **(Romans 8:28)**

I can't help but offer a teary-eyed but grateful smile in appreciation for this challenging journey and all that it's produced in me, through me and for me. It's all been for God's glory and Steve's honor.

As part of the *Suddenly Single* series, I penned this book dedicated to widows and widowers everywhere. I am a living witness that God can use your pain and turn it into purpose if you allow it. There's so much in store for you that goes beyond what you've experienced. I encourage you to use what you learned to not only help heal yourself but also to help heal others.

Honor God and your spouse by choosing to HEAL!

Now, go and be GREAT!

JAN MITCHELL

"My future is an amazing gift.
I will embrace it to
the fullest."

Anonymous

SUDDENLY *Single* WIDOW'S EDITION

Self-Worth Awakening

By: Jan Elizabeth Mitchell (Stansberry)

You thought that you broke me...
Like a trainer breaks a horse...
Like a scorned lover shatters glass...
Broke like your empty pockets...

You did.
You broke me...

You broke my low self-esteem from me...
You broke my tolerance for nonsense & weightless promises...
You broke my desperation for a relationship at any cost....Nah, not worth my peace!
You broke my fear of being alone...as I would rather be alone than miserable.
You broke the insanity of settling for less than I deserve...
When I am worthy of only the BEST!

You set me free.
Thank you.

Now, I am ALIVE to an authentic love that flows from inside me..through me..TO me...
I have a more profound sense of my strength, resilience, and purpose...my WORTH!
I love my voice..the essence that breathes life into my heart & soul....
And once, to yours...
An exquisite gift...your loss... a worthy other's gain...

I am comfortable in the skin that I am in...
I adore my tantalizing, almond-shaped eyes that are deep as my heart and my private sighs....

I cherish my for" giving" and for" living" heart...
I admire my courage... the strength to walk away...

To love me & to know me is a PRIVILEGE...not a right...
Yes, you broke me....and restored my sight...
Eyes wide open to my self-imposed limitations...
No more...I am FREE!
And I ain't mad at that because now I see...
I refuse to SETTLE...
Thank you for reawakening me to ME!

SUDDENLY *Single* **WIDOW'S EDITION**

REFERENCES:

What is Grief? (2016). *Mayo Clinic.* Retrieved from

https://www.mayoclinic.org/patient-visitor-guide/support-groups/what-is-grief

Zisook, Z., MD & Reynolds, III., C.F, MD. (2017). Complicated Grief. American Journal of Pyschotherapy. Retrieved from https://doi.org/10.1176/appi.focus.154S14

New Living Translation Version Bible. H. (2022). Bible Gateway Online.

https://www.biblegateway.com

7 Good Reasons to Cry: The Healing Property of Tears .(2011). *PsychCentral.* Retrieved from

https://psychcentral.com/blog/7-good-reasons-to-cry-the-healing-property-of-tears#1

Murray, B. (2002). Writing to heal: By helping people manage and learn from negative experiences, writing strengthens their immune systems as well as their minds. *American Psychological Association, 33*(6), 54. Retrieved from

 https://www.apa.org/monitor/jun02/writing

Rowett, A. (2015). The Prison of Unforgivness. *Bellevue Christian Counseling.* Retrieved from

https://bellevuechristiancounseling.com/articles/the-prison-of-unforgiveness.

SUDDENLY *Single* WIDOW'S EDITION

Merriam Webster (2022). Merriam Webster Dictionary Online. https://www.merriam-webster.com

Widow's Fire. (2022). Widows Fire. https://widowsfire.com

Differences Between Normal and Complicated Grief (2022, June 13). *VeryWell Health.* Retrieved from https://www.verywellhealth.com/grief-and-mourning-process-1132545

Getting Through Grief and Letting Go. (2020, Mar.22). *VeryWell Health.* Retrieved from https://www.verywellhealth.com/letting-go-of-grief-1132548

Forgiveness and Cancer (2018). *Clara Naum.* Retrieved from

https://www.claranaum.com/blog1/2018/7/19/forgiveness-and-cancer

Eight Keys to Forgiveness (2015). *Greater Good Magazine.* Retrieved from https://greatergood.berkeley.edu/article/item/eight_keys_to_forgiveness

How to Share STI Status, Why You Should, What to Say, More (2020). *Healthline.* Retrieved from https://www.healthline.com/health/healthy-sex/how-to-share-your-sti-std-status

ABOUT THE AUTHOR

Jan Mitchell

Jan Mitchell is a mom, certified identity trainer, and corporate trainer.

She is co-founder and co-host of "Well, Hades!!" a Christian based internet talk show. The show is dedicated to creating a safe, non-judgmental healing space for real people to have authentic conversations.

Jan is the CEO of the InnovativePR Co. and the forthcoming Non-Profit Organization, She Moves Forward, Inc. She Moves Forward, Inc. is an organization that assists widows in finding their new path after the death of their spouse.

She also currently sits on the board of directors for the

National Association of Healthcare Access Management (NAHAM) as the Midwest Regional Delegate. She has also written for NAHAM's" Access Management Journal."

She is the mother of three daughters, Korii, Zian and Ava. She is the glam-ma to one granddaughter, Liah.

She resides in Indianapolis, Indiana.

SUDDENLY *Single* **WIDOW'S EDITION**

CONTACT THE AUTHOR

🌐 **WEBSITE:**
www.theinnovativepr.co

✉ **EMAIL:**

jan.mitchell35@yahoo.com
info@theinnovativepr.co

Jan Mitchell

Made in United States
Orlando, FL
17 February 2024